1,40

THE BIBLE ON THE CHILDHOOD OF JESUS

L. HERMANS

The Bible on the Childhood of Jesus

Translated by H. J. J. VAUGHAN

SHEED AND WARD
LONDON AND MELBOURNE

FIRST PUBLISHED 1965
SHEED AND WARD LTD
33 MAIDEN LANE
LONDON W.C.2
AND
SHEED AND WARD PTY LTD
28 BOURKE STREET
MELBOURNE

Originally published as *De Bijbel over Jezus'
Geboorte en Jeugd*, J. J. Romen and Zonen,
Roermond (1962).

NIHIL OBSTAT: JOANNES M. T. BARTON, S.T.D., L.S.S.
    CENSOR DEPUTATUS

IMPRIMATUR: PATRITIUS CASEY,
    VIC. GEN.

WESTMONASTERII, DIE 22. VII. 65

The *Nihil obstat* and *Imprimatur* are a declaration that a book or
pamphlet is considered to be free from doctrinal or moral error.
It is not implied that those who have granted the *Nihil obstat*
and *Imprimatur* agree with the contents, opinions or statements
expressed.

This book is set in 12 pt. Linotype Granjon

*Made and printed in Great Britain by
William Clowes and Sons, Limited, London and Beccles*

Contents

Foreword

Iт sounds almost commonplace when we say that no time of year affects Christians as deeply as the Christmas season. No other feast is as popular as Christmas and Christian people in general observe it far more religiously than the central feast of Easter. It is a festival of joy, not only for Christians who keep it as the birthday of the Son of God, but also for many non-Christians who create a Christmas atmosphere with sprigs of holly and candlelight—a faint reflection maybe of the Light of Christmas. Through the ages, Christian artists and poets of all nations have repeatedly sought inspiration in the ancient bible stories about Jesus' birth and childhood. The crib, which we owe to Francis of Assisi, has familiarized us with the scene of the stable with its ox and its ass, with the figures of the shepherds and the adoration of the Magi.

There is an obvious link between this way of celebrating Christmas and the biblical details on the birth and childhood of Jesus contained in the first two chapters of Matthew and Luke's Gospels, to which the liturgy of Advent and Christmastide make frequent reference. But since the Middle Ages, Christian tradition has turned the spotlight on Christ's humanity, whereas ancient Christendom made Christ, the glorified Lord, the centre of its devotion. The simple story of Matthew and Luke was embroidered with mainly apocryphal details which gave the original childhood story an idyllic quality. Most Christians listen to these stories in their own homes, in the Christmas atmosphere surrounding tree and crib. Hence a tendency, then and now, to over-emphasize the human side of the Gospel's Christmas story, thereby missing part of its message. It is no disparagement of the religious value of such an approach to say in all sincerity that it has undoubtedly obscured the real meaning of the Evangelists and relegated it to the background of religious awareness.

To discover the powerful message of these gospel stories in their original perspective we must, for a moment, give up our all-to-human approach and do our utmost to grasp the real thoughts and meaning of the sacred authors—an effort which will turn these chapters into a veritable gold-mine of ancient Christian spirituality.

But the stories about Jesus' childhood also raise many scientific problems, some of them extending beyond the world of professional exegesis and therefore not to be treated with excessive technicality. Besides, the study of these problems can be beneficial to theology and biblical devotion.

This book sets out to acquaint the reader with the problems of biblical interpretation and to assist him in discovering the abundant religious themes and concepts of the childhood story. Although most readers will welcome this help, a quiet and attentive reading of the bible text itself remains all-important.

In compiling this work I have made ample use of the more recent literature. A special mention is due to: R. Laurentin, *Structure et Théologie de Luc i–ii*, Paris (1957); St. Lyonnet, *Le récit de l'Annonciation et la maternité divine de la Sainte Vierge*, Rome (1956); P. Gächter, *Maria im Erdenleben*, 3rd ed., Innsbruck (1955).

The reason why I wrote this book is my conviction that the centuries-old traditional Christmas celebrations can acquire a far deeper dimension if more and more Christians gain an insight into the actual meaning of the Evangelists to whom we owe the original Christmas story. In the process they will discover that the bible story about the child Jesus is anything but a children's story.

1

The Origin of the
Childhood Story*

ONE of the first things to consider is the origin of these narratives, and in this connection it should be stated from the outset that the stories about Jesus' birth and childhood were obviously not part of the earliest Christian preaching. Strange and unlikely though this contention may appear at first sight—after all, both Matthew and Luke devote the opening pages of their gospels to these narratives—it can be substantiated, principally by pointing to their absence in Mark and John, but also by making a study of the meaning of the term "gospel" in particular and of the Gospels in general.

For many the term "gospel" suggests primarily or perhaps even exclusively the four familiar books of gospels, though the connotation of "book" is one that the word "gospel" never has in the New Testament. Its usual significance could be described as "the glad tidings of the divine redemption which was made manifest in Jesus and introduces the new era",[1] in other words, the

* The footnote indices in the text refer to the notes at the back of this book, on p. 111.

5

redemptive message preached by Jesus himself, and more especially the good and joyful news spread by the apostles of the redemption which was made manifest in Jesus and was offered to mankind. Originally therefore it invariably means the living, spoken word of the preaching; and accordingly the original meaning of the title "evangelist" is: an itinerant preacher. (Cf. Acts xxi.8; Eph. iv.11; 2 Tim. iv.5.) It is only about the middle of the second century that Justin uses the word "gospel" in the sense of a book containing the written deposit of the living, spoken gospel; and consequently we see that since the third century the term "evangelists" denotes the authors or writers of the four books of gospels.

In fact also the written gospel comes after the spoken gospel. In the beginning there was only the word. Between the death and resurrection of Jesus and the definitive edition of our oldest gospels (Mark, Matthew and Luke) there was an interval of at least thirty years of mainly verbal preaching. The written gospels came into being at the time when Jesus' first eye- and ear-witnesses were growing scarce. The apostles, as first-hand witnesses, had no need of books in their preaching and religious instruction; they were able to draw on their personal recollections and experiences. The martyrdom of these first witnesses saw the origin of the gospels as we know them (probably along with various other ventures alluded to in the prologue to Luke's Gospel, Luke i.1–4). They

6

were above all the deposit of the preaching and teaching of the apostolic witnesses, and served their successors as an aid in their work as preachers and catechists.

If, therefore, the oldest gospels are to be regarded as the echo, the written record, of the verbal preaching of the apostles, it will be worth considering what they spoke about to the first Christians. In the Acts of the Apostles, especially the first part, there are several brief outline sketches of these ancient sermons extant. (Cf. ii.22–39; iii.12–26; iv.8–12; v.30–32; x.36–43; xiii.17–41.) It is striking that in these passages the apostles always speak as witnesses of the reality which they themselves have seen, heard and experienced. The central truth they proclaim is Jesus' resurrection from the dead and his exaltation. The conclusion of Peter's sermon at the first Pentecost: "Let all the house of Israel therefore know assuredly that God has made him both Lord and Christ, this Jesus whom you crucified" (Acts ii.36) forms the central evidence, and to it were added the other stories about the finding of the empty grave, about the seizing and condemnation of Jesus, which were partly intended for the instruction of the faithful. Gradually the life, miracles and teaching of Jesus also found a place in this instruction. (Cf. Acts x.34–43.) But the life of Jesus never went beyond the activities of John the Baptist and John's baptism in the River Jordan. In the oldest gospel-plan the Baptist always stands on the threshold of the Gospel. We observe therefore that the subject-matter of the oldest preaching and teaching is in fact restricted to what we term Jesus' public life and that the redemptive value of Jesus' resurrection is brought into special relief. The requirements laid down by Peter for those likely to qualify as successor to Judas, the traitor, are a pointer in the same direction:

> So one of the men who have accompanied us during all the time that the Lord Jesus went in and out among us, beginning from the baptism of John until the day when he was taken up from us—one of these men must become with us a witness to his resurrection. [Acts i.21–2.]

No wonder that Mark's Gospel—according to ancient tradition and its own textual evidence closely related to and in part the deposit of Peter's preaching in Rome—opens with the activities of John the Baptist and closes with the death, resurrection and ascension of Jesus. This gospel appears to elaborate on Peter's address in the house of Cornelius, a Roman officer, at Caesarea. (Acts x.34–43.) St John's Gospel also follows the ancient layout of sermon and gospel: immediately after the prologue (John i.1–18) the author describes the Baptist's activities by the River Jordan; Matthew and Luke follow the other evangelists, commencing at Chapter 3.

We find that there is no place in these old layouts for what preceded Jesus' public life. The preaching makes frequent reference to Jesus' descent from David (cf. Acts iii.30; xii.23; Rom. i.3) and it is common knowledge that he was about thirty years old when he began his public life (cf. Luke iii.23), but there is no mention anywhere of his birth and childhood and the quiet years in Nazareth. Nor do we find anything about it in Paul's letters. All this seems quite easy to explain. In the first place, the apostles are not first-hand witnesses of what happened in the hidden period of Jesus' life; they have not personally taken part in these events. In the second, it can in general be said that the earliest preaching was not interested in the details of Jesus' human family circumstances. Its aim was not to point out the humanity, the human origin of the Lord. There were no doubts on that score: he had been seen in the flesh and been listened to; he had been addressed, persecuted and executed. Its interest lay in demonstrating his supernatural mission and function and in making the first listeners aware of the mystery of his supernatural being. We, modern-day Christians, see in our minds the formidable problem that God truly became man and find it rather difficult to visualize God on earth, whereas the first Christians of Jerusalem and Palestine were confronted with the unbelievable fact that the man from despised Nazareth, whose execution on the cross made his mission seem such a hopeless failure, was exalted at the right hand of God and made Lord and

Christ. (Acts ii.33–6.) We can therefore understand that the apostles' preaching which began
after the first Pentecost did not stress the
humanity, the human origin and birth of Jesus,
the Christ, the Lord, but rather the divine Spirit
which was active in him in a special way. They
obviously emphasized the very points that made it
clear he was more than man and had to be
measured by other standards than those of
ordinary mortals; and that in his greatness he
transcended all purely human proportions. In this
connection the official witnesses point especially
to the Resurrection or, to use their own, far more
expressive words, to the fact that God has raised
him from the dead; thus strongly contrasting
God's life-giving activity towards Jesus of Nazareth with the life-taking actions of the Jews who
put him to death on the cross.

On reflection, the most wonderful part of the
stories about Jesus' birth and childhood seems to
be the fact that they exist at all and that they are
in our possession. Between the events of the childhood story and their recording in the present
edition of the childhood gospels of Matthew and
Luke lies an interval of at least two or more
generations, which is twice as long as it took for
the events of the other gospel tidings to be
recorded in writing. These reflections have further
brought out that in those days the preaching
apparently attached no importance to Jesus' childhood. Moreover, the traditions about Jesus' hidden

life were not confirmed by the multitude's knowledge of them, as were a large number of the
reports about his public life. Anyhow, these childhood stories occupy a place apart in the primitive
gospel and even in the whole New Testament
literature. They lie rather on the periphery of the
"Gospel" proper. Maybe they are the answer to a
subsequent interest on the part of the faithful,
whose understandable—because very human—
and perhaps even more-or-less profane curiosity
impelled them to seek further information on the
Lord's hidden life.[2] It is good to note this before
taking a closer look at the gospel stories about
Jesus' childhood. The oldest preaching was concerned with the Lord's public life and death and
more especially his resurrection, with the Easter
event and its redemptive significance. It was only
later, though still in the apostolic era, that the
interest in the hidden life, the quiet years in
Nazareth, the childhood and birth of Jesus, the
Christmas event, became apparent.[3] It would be
intriguing to follow the development of this
interest through the centuries and trace the
gradual shifting of the emphasis in the preaching,
in Christian art and in the religious observance of
the faithful, from the Easter event to that of
Christmas.

Our present knowledge of Jesus' childhood
years derives from what the first two chapters of
Matthew and Luke's gospels have preserved for
us. The content and nature of these stories refer

us in the last instance to Jesus' family circle where
they were stored up and pondered. One important
source was presumably Mary who alone witnessed
many of the events narrated. It was the evangelists
Matthew and Luke who somehow collated these
reminiscences and reflections; in the process it
seemed to them that the human birth and surroundings of Jesus contained various data which
threw light on the Lord's wonderful and
mysterious personality and made it clear that he
was the long-awaited Messiah, the Son of God.
These data therefore fitted quite well into the drift
of the oldest preaching and could easily be included by way of introduction in the two books
of gospels—the written deposit of the ancient,
verbal gospel.

Marie-Joseph Lagrange suggests yet another
reason why Luke may have included the childhood story in the gospel:

A custom had grown up in the East of giving
to sovereigns the title of Saviour or God—
Saviour, and by that very fact an all-important
significance was attached to their birth; for if a
sovereign was entitled to be called a god it
could only be because of his divine origin, and
this divine origin was consecrated and made
manifest to all men by means of his birth.
Already as early as the year 238 BC, the birth
of King Ptolemy had been described as the day
on which all mankind began to receive many

benefits. In the case of Antiochus of Commagene (from 69 to about 34 BC) his birth and coronation were said to be divine epiphanies or, as we say, manifestations. It was about the same time that Virgil was making known to the world that a ruler was to appear who should restore the golden age, the beginnings of which were to be found in a childhood that was miraculous. Finally, in the year 9 BC Paulus Fabius Maximus, the proconsul of Roman Asia, made a proposal to the people of his province that they should count the birthday of Augustus as their New Year's Day. In his proclamation he said: "It is a question whether we derive more pleasure or more profit from the birthday of the most divine Caesar, for it is a day that might well be compared to the beginning of everything—if not the beginning of all being, at all events the source of all our benefit. For this day has restored all that was in decay and all that had fallen into misfortune; and a new appearance has been put upon the entire world, which would have perished but for the birth of Caesar who is the blessing of all men." Note that it is precisely the birthday of Caesar Augustus which gives to the world the beginning of good tidings, or εὐαγγέλια (gospels) as the Greek puts it. And when a prince succeeded to the throne, his accession was looked on as a second and further announcement of good tidings: thus, when Nero came to the imperial throne in the year 54, he was proclaimed to the world as the hope of the universe.

Is it Luke's intention, then, to imitate the official protocol? Perhaps; but if he does so it is with a tremendous difference. It was rather his intention to accept the challenge thrown down by these proud monarchs or by their flattering courtiers when he claimed the title of Saviour for a child born in a crib, a child who at that time had few to pay him homage. And events have proved that Luke was in the right, for it is from the birthday of Jesus that we count this new era, which, by contrast with that unknown time when the world first came into being, is like a new creation. Men have not begun to count time, as the proconsul desired, from the birthday of Augustus, who did no more than restore a social order that has long since passed away.[4]

One final remark about Luke's childhood story. The childhood story in general has already been shown to have a character all its own within the framework of the gospels; and this is further underlined and confirmed by the peculiarity with which it has in many respects been endowed by Luke. It comprises the first two chapters of his gospel, apart from the prologue. (Luke i.1–4.) Anyone reading Luke's Gospel in Greek will, on passing beyond the foreword, make a remarkable discovery similar to that of one crossing the border between two entirely different countries. From the pure, refined Greek of the elegantly written prologue he will suddenly, at Luke i.5, pass into a story of Semitic colouring and appearance: a story which in language, style and concepts has a very Jewish and Old-Testament flavour. The text largely retains this character up to Luke ii.40, and in a slightly lesser degree up to and including Luke ii.52, i.e., up to Chapter 3 which opens with the activities of the Baptist—the normal gateway to the Gospel proper. This Semitic colouring of language and style was in the past held to be a reason for regarding it as an interpolation, as if the childhood history had only been added to Luke's Gospel at a later date. Most exegetes nowadays have gone back on such radical hypotheses and recognize that these chapters form part of Luke's work, at least in its definitive edition. For that matter, there is no unanimous explanation for this Semitic character. There are some who consider these Semitisms to be an imitation of the language of the Septuagint (the Greek translation of the Old Testament by the Seventy): in their view, Luke is showing his literary artistry by imitating the biblical language of the Septuagint in his sacred narrative. Others regard them as translating Semitisms, and are of the opinion that for these stories Luke has used one or more Hebrew or Aramaic documents (possibily already translated into Greek before he did so) and incorporated them in the definitive edition of his gospel, perhaps with slight adaptations.

The arguments for a written Hebrew original seem to be finding more and more acceptance with the exegetes. Luke, the Hellenist and Gentile converted to Christianity, who presumably hailed from Antioch in Syria, can hardly be the original author of these two chapters. The local Palestinian colouring of these narratives points to a Jewish-Christian who was familiar with Judea, Jerusalem and the Jewish temple. The Semitic style, still recognizable in the Greek text of Luke i–ii, puts us in mind of someone who has Hebrew or Aramaic as his mother tongue. Moreover, we continually savour the spirit and devoutness of pious Jewry which is aware of being tied to temple and law, and strongly emphasizes the Old Testament, Jewish laws and customs adhered to by Jesus' family, such as the presentation in the temple and the ascent to the temple. The hymns of Mary, Zechariah and Simeon, spread over these chapters, breathe the spirit of the Old Testament. All this seems to indicate that the original narrator of these tales was not a Greek but a Jew, who went over to Christianity and should perhaps be sought in the priestly circles of Jerusalem. In Acts vi.7 Luke mentions that many of the Jewish priests in Jerusalem were converted.

In any event, we must be convinced that Luke's childhood gospel bears a strikingly Old-Testament character, which will prove exceedingly important for the interpretation, whether as a whole or in part.

2

A Comparison Between Matthew 1–2 and Luke 1–2

THE previous chapter has given an insight into
the unique character of the stories about Jesus'
birth and childhood and their place apart within
the framework of the Gospel proper. A comparison between Matthew's childhood stories and
those of Luke will bring out above all the
character, spirit and atmosphere peculiar to them
in Matthew and Luke respectively. There is agreement between Matt. i–ii and Luke i–ii on a few
very important points, including the virgin conception, the imposition of the name Jesus in
accordance with the words of the angel, the birth
in Bethlehem and the childhood years in Nazareth. For that matter, these points of similarity
tie up with the data of the fourth gospel. (Cf. John
i.13–14; i.46 and vi.42; vii.42; i.45–8.) But the
differences stand out much more than the similari-
ties and accordingly they will be discussed at
length.

1. *Difference of content and matter*

This is undoubtedly the most striking difference of all.[5] Matthew starts off with a rather artificial genealogy (i.1–17) of Jesus Christ, son of David, son of Abraham, built on the figure seven—a sacred one for Jews; cf. Matt. i.17: "So all the generations from Abraham to David were fourteen generations, and from David to the deportation to Babylon fourteen generations, and from the deportation to Babylon to the Christ fourteen generations." Thus, after three sets of fourteen generations or six times seven generations, the coming of the Messiah will introduce the seventh period and the fullness of time. The purpose of this genealogy is to show that Jesus' messianic character is vouched for by his origin, and to this end it links him with the most important bearers of the messianic promises: Jesus is the son of Abraham who received the promise that by him all the families of the earth would bless themselves (Gen. xii.1–3); he is also the son of David who, in Nathan's familiar prophecy (2 Sam. vii.4–16), was given the pledge that his offspring would reign for ever as God's chosen people. These are the means by which Matthew, a converted Palestinian Jew, tries to prove from the Scriptures that Jesus is "he who is to come" (Matt. xi.3) and to give his Jewish compatriots the emphatic assurance that the promises to the forefathers have been fulfilled in him.[6] The rest of the first chapter gives an hieratic account of the doubt that God's intervention in the life of Joseph has created regarding his marriage, and of the way it was removed. (Matt. i.18–25.) The real meaning of this passage will be closely studied in the next section.

There then follows in Matt. ii a series of events from Jesus' childhood, vividly and dramatically narrated in four self-contained stories: the visit of the Magi from the East, at that time regarded by Palestinian Jews as the cradle of magic and wisdom (ii.1–12)[7]; the flight into Egypt (ii.13–15); the massacre of the innocents in and around Bethlehem (ii.16–18); and finally the return from Egypt and the definitive settlement in Nazareth (ii.19–23). The striking part of all these stories is the strong prophetic strain; they are crystallized round an explicit prophetic quotation; Matt. i.22–3:

> All this took place to fulfil what the Lord had spoken by the prophet: "Behold, a virgin shall conceive and bear a son, and his name shall be called Emmanuel" (which means, God is with us).

In Matt. ii.1–12 strangers from the East declare that they have seen the star of the newly born King of the Jews in the eastern sky. It seems quite possible that the evangelist finds a link here with the ancient oracle of Balaam, in which a messianic ruler from the dynasty of David is greeted under the sign of a star (a royal symbol in the ancient East): "I see him, but not now; I behold him, but

not nigh; a star shall come forth out of Jacob, and
a sceptre shall rise out of Israel." (Num. xxiv.17.)
When King Herod subsequently calls the scribes
together to learn from them the birthplace of the
new king, they read to him from the prophet
Micah: "But you, O Bethlehem Ephrathah, who
are little to be among the clans of Judah, from you
shall come forth for me one who is to be ruler in
Israel." (Mic. v.2.) Here Scripture becomes a
signpost to the birthplace of the Messiah. The
enumeration of the presents in Matt. ii.11 looks
like an implicit reference to Isa. lx.6:

"A multitude of camels shall cover you, the
young camels of Midian and Ephah; all those
from Sheba shall come. They shall bring gold
and frankincense, and shall proclaim the praise
of the Lord." [Cf. Ps. lxxii.15; Jer. vi.20.]

In painting the sombre scene of the massacre of
the infants perpetrated by the embittered Herod
in and around Bethlehem, the evangelist evokes
the picture of Rachel, the ancient matriarch, as
the prophet Jeremiah once let her weep over the
people of Israel going into exile:

"A voice is heard in Ramah, lamentation and
bitter weeping. Rachel is weeping for her children; she refuses to be comforted for her children, because they are not." [Jer. xxxi.15.]

In Matt. ii.15 we read a quotation from Hos.
xi.1:

[He] remained there until the death of Herod.
This was to fulfil what the Lord had spoken
by the prophet, "Out of Egypt have I called
my son."[8]

According to Matt. ii.23 the settlement in Nazareth is the fulfilment of a prophecy: "He shall be
called a Nazarene." Remarkably, this prophecy
can nowhere be found in this form in the Old
Testament, nor has an adequate explanation for
it been forthcoming as yet. Some authors are
reminded of Judges xiii.7 and assume that what
Matthew means is that Jesus will be a Nazarite
like Samson (one who is consecrated to the service
of God); others think he is making a pun on the
Hebrew word *neser*, meaning "shoot", which
appears in the messianic passage Isa. xi.1 and in
Isa. liii.2. The most likely explanation is probably
that this passage which closes Matthew's childhood gospel, reflects his overall thoughts on what
the Prophets in general have said about the Messiah, especially about his simple, humble and
despised origin.[9]

Further on I shall revert to these explicit Old-
Testament quotations in Matt. i–ii, but there is no
harm in observing here and now that the events
narrated by Matthew are obviously not all that
important in themselves; if he relates them it is
because they constitute the fulfilment of a prophecy. It is a well-known fact that this interest is
typical of the whole of Matthew's Gospel,[10] which

is written for a Christian public that heard the Old Testament being read out and expounded year in year out in the Jewish synagogues. These quotations from the Old Testament give his stories a sacred character and make them suitable for discussion at religious meetings. They have, moreover, a pronouncedly apologetic significance: in Jesus of Nazareth the Old-Testament prophecies have been fulfilled; he completes the old redemptive economy; he is the crowning, the keystone, of the old, preparatory redemptive order; he is the one who gives meaning to the history of God's chosen people, whose duty it is, therefore, to become a Christian people.

The matter of *Luke*'s first two chapters differs considerably from the content of Matt. i–ii which I have just sketched.[11] Luke is an erudite man with a classical and literary education, of pagan origin (Col. iv.10–14), presumably from Antioch in Syria. The place and time of his conversion to Christianity are unknown but, if the version of Codex D of Acts xi.28 is correct, he joined Antioch's community of converts from paganism at quite an early date.[12] In Col. iv.14 Paul calls him: "Luke the beloved physician." Like many doctors at that time he led a cosmopolitan life and thus we see him going about the cities of the ancient East as the travelling companion of Paul, who may have been one of his patients. (Acts xvi.10–17; xx.5–15; xxi.1–18.) He also accom-

panies his revered master when, after his arrest in
Jerusalem, he was sent a prisoner from Caesarea
to Rome. (Acts xxvii.1–28, 16.) Luke's plan is to
write "the history of the Christian beginnings",
one great work in two parts: the history (or
rather, perhaps, the biography) of Christ (Luke's
Gospel) and the history of the origin and the early
development of the church (the Acts of the
Apostles). As far as his gospel is concerned, his
aim is to write a biography of Jesus. (Luke i.3.)
Indeed, he intends to give more than the echo
and deposit of the religious teaching about Jesus'
life and preaching, his death and resurrection. In
other words, he wants to give more than Mark
and Matthew offer in their gospels; his plan—
and in this respect he undoubtedly stands alone
among the evangelists—is to write history, and
that after the style of the classical biographers of
his day, to whom a correct characterization of
their hero is more important than an accurate
marshalling of the actual facts. To this end Luke
has drawn from all available and attainable
sources in order that he may be as well informed
as possible on the life of his hero.[13] In the final
analysis his plan has failed, chiefly because the
material at his disposal was largely unsuitable for
the composition of a biography in the true sense.
It consisted in the main of the type of material
(Jesus' sayings and events from his life) which
was used in preaching and religious instruction,[14]
activities not unduly interested in the biographi-

cal, topographical and chronological aspects of the life of Jesus. But if he was unable, on this account, to write a "Life of Jesus", his efforts in this direction at least enabled him to acquire new data about Jesus' life in general and his birth and childhood in particular.[15]

Mention has already been made (p. 15ff.) of the opinion commonly held among exegetes that Luke found the narrative of the first two chapters of his gospel, with the exception of course of the prologue i.1–4, in more or less finished form, in an ancient document which was the Greek translation of a Semitic and probably Hebrew original and incorporated it in his gospel with slight adaptations. It comprised two cycles of narratives, remarkably similar descriptions of the birth and childhood of John the Baptist and Jesus. In turn he deals with the annunciation of John's birth to his father Zechariah (i.5–25) and the annunciation of Jesus' birth to Mary (i.26–38). These strongly parallel narratives are concluded with the account of Mary's visitation to Elizabeth. (i.39–56.) Next he relates John's birth and circumcision (i.57–80), which has its counterpart in the narration of Jesus' birth and circumcision. (ii.1–21.) These two nativity stories are concluded by the account of the presentation of Jesus (ii.22–40) and his finding in the temple at Jerusalem (ii.41–52).

This synopsis of the content of Luke i–ii clearly shows that Luke surpasses his fellow evangelist Matthew by far. His supremacy is complete as regards the childhood stories of John the Baptist which are entirely lacking in Matthew; but apart from this, Luke's narratives about Jesus' childhood are more numerous and they cover different events.

However, the difference between Matthew and Luke's childhood gospels is not only objective and, therefore, mainly quantitative; it is also qualitative—indeed this is far greater and more pronounced though perhaps less striking, as the sequel will show.

2. *Difference of main characters*

This heading should really be amended right away, for *the* main character in both Matthew and Luke is undoubtedly Jesus. The interest of both is obviously directed to the child; both authors want to show us clearly who Jesus really is. In the annunciation stories the accent lies not on the person to whom the message is addressed— Zechariah and Mary. A close examination of the content of both messages reveals that it is not primarily the parents who are discussed and revered, but the children. These messages are not merely the announcement that the parents are to expect the blessing of a child, but rather that their children will be blessed children who are to play a decisive role in God's redemptive plan, now nearing its climax. The first child will be great before the Lord and go before the Messiah in the spirit and power of the prophet Elijah; the second will reign over the House of Jacob for ever and be seated on the throne of his father David. John will be the forerunner of the Messiah and make ready for the Lord a people prepared; Jesus will be the one who is to come, the heir of King David to whom God swore an oath that of his reign there would be no end. Both messages are pre-eminently messianic; they refer to the messianic child whose arrival introduces the long-awaited redemptive era.

But when we study the figures who occupy important though secondary places, we observe a new and remarkable difference between Matt. i–ii and Luke i–ii.

Matthew's childhood gospel can be classified as a story about Joseph in the sense that it is not Mary but Joseph who stands in the forefront.

Although Matt. i.18ff. clearly indicates that Joseph is not Jesus' natural father, Matthew nevertheless gives Joseph's genealogy (cf. Matt. i.16) and not Mary's. Matt. i.18–25 relates the virgin conception from Joseph's point of view. The explicit quotation of the Emmanuel-prophecy from Isa. ii.14 in the very centre of this passage would justify our expectation to see Mary occupy an important position, at least in this episode; but it is not so. It is true that her virginity is explicitly mentioned (cf. Matt. i.18, 20, 23) and even strongly emphasized (i.25), but for Mary herself no direct light is thrown upon it; it is almost as if her virginity is of more importance to Jesus than it is to her. On closer examination it even seems possible that Matthew only takes a side-long glance at the virgin conception. The main attention in this passage falls rather on Joseph's legal fatherhood, as a word-for-word translation of Matt. i.20–21 will show: "Joseph, son of David, do not hesitate to take Mary, your spouse, to you; for there is no doubt that what is born in her is the work of the Holy Ghost; yet, she shall bring forth a son whom you must call Jesus; for he shall set his people free from their sins." This pericope culminates in Joseph's fatherhood: God's Spirit may be the architect of this miraculous conception; but nevertheless in God's plan Joseph, too, has a role to play in this miraculous birth. He sees his own marriage plans thwarted by a special intervention from God and accordingly he wants to withdraw in holy fear and trembling, to leave his bride free for God alone. But he receives a message from God that he will have to play the role of legal father towards this child; and therefore he is to take the mother of the child to him (in other words, he must proceed with the home-coming) and name the child.[16]

The pericope about the visit of the Magi speaks of "the child and his mother" (Matt. ii.11)—an expression that recurs a few times in the subsequent stories (cf. Matt. ii.14, 20–21)—but this very formula indicates that the attention is particularly directed to the child. Another point worth noting is that Matt. ii.6 breaks off the explicit quotation from Mic. v.1 at the moment when the prophet is about to speak of the mother of the Messiah.[17] Finally it should be pointed out that Matt. i–ii thrice mentions a dream to Joseph (cf. Matt. i.20–23; ii.13, 19–20), whereas there is no mention anywhere of a vision or anything like it to Mary. All this justifies our description of Matt. i–ii as a story about Joseph.

There is just as much justification for calling Luke i–ii a story about Mary. Indeed this is so obvious that a few brief remarks will suffice. Joseph does not step into the foreground at all here and he is only mentioned a few times by name. (Cf. Luke i.27; ii.4, 16.) On the occasion of Jesus' presentation in the temple Luke ii.27 speaks of "his parents", and after the venerable Simeon's canticle, the author says that "his father and mother were dumbfounded by what was said of him" (Luke ii.33)[18]; but after Simeon has blessed them both, he addresses Mary in particular (Luke ii.34–5) and tells her a sword shall pierce her, dividing and rending her body.[19] The pericope on the finding also speaks about Jesus' parents (Luke ii.41–3), but it is Mary who turns to the twelve-year-old boy and gives evidence of her anxious search for her lost son: "Behold, your father and I sought you with sorrow" (Luke ii.48), whilst Jesus tells her in his strange and incomprehensible answer (Luke ii.50)—Jesus' only recorded childhood saying—that he must be in the house of *his Father*, thereby indicating who is his real father. (Luke ii.49.) As we have seen, Matt. i–ii mentions a few of Joseph's visionary dreams; in Luke i–ii the angel Gabriel takes God's message of messianic joy to Mary, who at the same time receives a new name: "blessed", "privileged", "full of grace" (Luke i.28) in the same way that those who are assigned a special function or mission in God's redemptive plans are given a new name on that very account. A further point of interest is that in Luke we can read a twofold blessing of Mary: one by Elizabeth who calls her blessed for carrying Jesus in her womb (Luke i.42) and because of her great faith (i.45), the other contained in the hymn of praise—which the author makes Mary recite—predicting that all generations shall call her blessed because of the great things God has done to her. (Luke 1.47–8.) Finally, we observe that in Luke's text Mary's virginity acquires a positive meaning for her too[20]; we see her virginity turn from a fact (Luke i.27) into a problem (i.34), and grow from a problem into a positive way of life, into a bondage in faithful and exclusive submission to God's word and to him alone: "Behold the handmaiden of the Lord: let it be done unto me according to thy word." (i.38.)

3. *Difference of geographical accent*

In this respect Matt. i–ii can be called a Bethlehem-story. Mary and Joseph do not travel from

Nazareth to Bethlehem as we read in Luke (ii.1ff.); they are already there. The Magi journey from the East to Jerusalem, but they are directed to Bethlehem, for that is where the prophecy points. (Matt. ii.1–12.) After the return from Egypt. Joseph wants to go back to Bethlehem, but when he learns that Herod's son Archelaus is reigning in Judea he is afraid to return there and, warned in a dream, he emigrates to the region of Galilee and settles in Nazareth. (Matt. ii.22–3.)

In Luke i–ii the nativity in Bethlehem, as well as Mary's visitation to Elizabeth, is to be regarded as an interlude in the overall narrative. Joseph and Mary are in Nazareth (cf. Luke i.26ff.) and always end up by returning there (cf. Luke 1.56; ii.39, 51). We also note that Jerusalem occupies a large place in Luke i–ii: his childhood gospel opens in the temple of Jerusalem (Luke i.5ff.) and there too lies the climax of the childhood stories; cf. the presentation in the temple (ii.22–38) and the finding in the temple with the explicit statement: "Did you not know that I *must* be in my Father's house?" (ii.41–50.) In fact, that applies to Luke's Gospel as a whole: a mythical force drives Jesus' life, as it were, towards the holy city, which is to be the scene of his suffering and his victory.[21] We can conclude from this that Luke i–ii can be classified as a Nazareth- and Jerusalem-story.

4. *Difference of "atmosphere"*

In character, atmosphere and tone also the two childhood stories offer a strong contrast. Matthew's is woebegone; the events he relates are sombre and full of menace. There hangs over his story the strain of persecution and gripping fear. After the genealogy he mentions the painful uncertainty which has arisen in Joseph regarding his marriage. The flight to Egypt in the depth of night puts the damper on the visit from the Magi. The anger of Herod when he sees himself deceived by these Easterners is vented on the children of Bethlehem and the surrounding district, and the author lets us hear the wailings of Rachel, the matriarch, weeping over her children and refusing to be consoled because they are no more. After Herod's death the holy family returns from Egypt but dares not settle in Bethlehem for fear of Archelaus, who has become Ethnarch of Judea in their absence, and accordingly they move out to Nazareth in Galilee. Everywhere we meet a sombre atmosphere of anxiety and persecution, heralding the coming rejection of the Messiah by his people. Jesus is portrayed as a new Moses, who has to endure the same persecutions as the Moses of the Book of Exodus and of the Jewish apocryphal history of Moses.[22] Thus these first two chapters fit nicely into the framework of Matthew's Gospel as a whole. Jesus fulfils the prophecies and the redemptive promises of old; he completes the Old Testament, but on the day when "the one

31

who is to come" appears at last, the Jews do not bother about him. Pagans tell them he has come; the Jews know where he is to be born and show the Magi the way to Bethlehem but they themselves stir not a foot in that direction; only Herod has plans to adore the child, though in reality they are but murder plans. One day the Jews will succeed in killing the Messiah, but even when their own people (the watchers at the sepulchre) give evidence for the Resurrection, the divine confirmation of Jesus' mission, the leaders of the Jewish people remain obstinate in their rejection of the Messiah and try bribery to twist the actual facts. (Matt. xxviii.11–15.) After this refusal of the *Chosen People* to accept Jesus' messianic mission there follows the last conversation of "him to whom all authority has been given" with the eleven disciples, in which they are instructed to make disciples of *all nations*. (Matt. xxviii.16–20.)

By contrast Luke tells a happy tale, scintillating with joy at the coming of the Messiah; an idyllic and "melodious" story in which we are carried from one story to another. Filled with the Spirit, Zechariah praises Yahweh, the God of Israel: "Blessed be the Lord God of Israel, for he has visited and redeemed his people." (Luke i.67ff.) Mary sings her magnificat "My soul magnifies the Lord, and my spirit rejoices in God, my Saviour." (Luke i.46ff.) The angels sing the Gloria: "Glory to God in the highest, and on earth peace among men with whom he is pleased." (Luke ii.14.) And when Simeon takes the child in his arms in the temple, he blesses God and sings: "Lord, now lettest thou thy servant depart in peace..." (Luke ii.28–32.) These joyful sounds that start around the baby's crib will go on sounding right through the whole of Luke's Gospel (cf. Luke v.26; x.17; xiii.17; xviii.43; xix.37; xxiv.41–52), and the *Bible de Jérusalem* rightly remarks: "A sound of singing souls rings right through this hopeful work, which opens with the *Gloria in excelsis Deo* and finds its worthy conclusion in the scene of the apostles blessing God in the temple." (Luke xxiv.53.)

5. *Dream and message*

Finally, there is a difference in the form of contact between God and man in the two childhood stories. Matthew obviously prefers God's contact in the form of a dream. Three times we read that "an angel of the Lord appeared to Joseph in a dream". (Matt. i.20; ii.13–19; cf. also ii.12, 22; xxvii.19.) The ancients held dreams to be man's means of contact with the world of God and the spirits, and they often regarded them as a revelation of things to come and of other hidden matters. The Israelites also frequently regard them as predictions (Gen. xxxvii.5–10; xl; xli; Judges vii.13ff; Dan. ii.1; iv.2) or as revelations of hidden truths (1 Sam. xxviii.5, 15). Occasionally God also reveals himself in dreams to the Prophets. (Num. xii.6; Dan. vii.1; Joel iii.1.) Some of the Old-Testament authors are critical of dreams. In Ecclus. xxxiv.1ff., for instance, we read:

> Dreams give wings to fools; as one who catches at a shadow and pursues the wind, so is he who gives heed to dreams. The vision of dreams is this against that, the likeness of a face confronting a face ... divinations and omens and dreams are folly, and like a woman in travail the mind has fancies. Unless they are sent from the most High as a visitation, do not give your mind to them. For dreams have deceived many and those who put their hope in them have failed.

The prophet Jeremiah satirizes the dreams of the false prophets, saying:

> "I have dreamed. I have dreamed!" How long shall there be lies in the heart of the prophets who prophesy lies ... What has straw in common with wheat? [Jer. xxiii.25ff.]

An adept at receiving nightly visions is Joseph, the son of the patriarch Jacob, detested by his brothers who flatly call him "the dreamer". These dream stories can be regarded as a definite form of the narrative art of the ancient Easterner, with typical qualities all its own. Their natural home is in the sphere of the nocturnal rest; the visionary usually does not speak, he just watches and listens; the content of the dream often relates to the recipient, occasionally to the future of God's chosen people.

There are no dreams in Luke's Gospel, which gives women a bigger place in the history of Jesus' life than Matthew's; this is why it is so striking that he fails to mention the wife of Pilate who, according to Matt. xxvii.19, "has suffered much over him [Jesus] today in a dream". In his second book, the Acts of the Apostles, Luke accords a wide place to prophecy and vision in the life of the young church, but there again dreams are not mentioned. From these and other details we can deduce that, for one reason or another, he has kept his distance from the dream as a means of contacting God. His literary process is the annunciation. In dream and annunciation alike it is God who takes the initiative to contact man, but there are differences, too. The one who receives the message is not asleep but wide awake, and this allows a conversation, an interplay of question and answer. Mostly no further explanation is needed once the message has been delivered; all is clear before the messenger leaves the scene. The gist of the message is usually of general interest and concerns the redemption of God's people or of mankind.

The universal importance of the coming of the Messiah for the redemption of all peoples has probably induced the author of Luke i–ii to model his narrative on the annunciations in the Old Testament, in which "the angel of Yahweh" often plays a part. Some exegetes feel there are reasons for assuming that he had definite Old-Testament annunciation stories in mind when he started to describe the annunciations to Zechariah and to Mary. Thus they refer to the annunciation of the angel to Abraham and Sarah (Gen. xviii), to Manoah, Samson's father (Judges xiii), and to Gideon (Judges vi). It will be no easy matter to get certainty on this point, especially because most of these annunciation stories reveal a fixed plan. But as a general observation the author of Luke's childhood story could be said to be more likely to have had the annunciation of a miraculous birth in mind.

How to explain all these differences? We are faced with two divergent, independent narratives from two different authors, each with his own sources of information, motives and circle of readers. The fact that both Matthew and Luke—and only they—precede their description of Jesus' public life with a story of his birth and childhood does not permit us to conclude either that they are dependent on each other or that they have both drawn from a common source. The differences of content and quality are too great for that. Both give but a small selection from the events surrounding the birth and infancy of Jesus (and of the Baptist). Not a single passage is common to both, not even Jesus' birth: Matthew does not really narrate this, he rather mentions—or better still, assumes—it in a subordinate clause. (ii.1.) If

Luke had known Matthew's narrative, we could have expected him to incorporate the adoration of the Magi, the first fruits from the pagan world, in his gospel which was destined for Christian converts from paganism. Both are, therefore, independent of each other and go back to two independent traditions. Hence the difficulty of making the two narratives harmonize. Luke ii.39ff. gives the impression that the return of the holy family to Nazareth takes place immediately after the presentation of Jesus in the temple, forty days after his birth. Matthew appears to present the facts in a different way: chronologically the coming of the Magi certainly falls after the presentation in the temple; moreover, we must add to these forty days the number of years or months of the stay in Egypt. Only then can there—according to Matthew—be any question of the return to Nazareth in Galilee mentioned in Luke ii.39. There is no need for us to seek a contradiction here, nor should we try to harmonize these two narratives completely. On the contrary, it will be better to allow each childhood story its own nature and to evaluate it on its own merits.

3

The Structure of
Luke 1–2

1. *Scenes*

Having dwelt at some length on Matt. i–ii in
the preceding chapter, I shall devote the following
pages mainly to Luke i–ii.

The first two chapters of Luke could be compared with a dramatic play consisting of a
number of separate scenes. Christian iconography
has distinguished them from of old and given
them individual portrayal. They are to a great
extent constructed on the same fixed, yet flexibly
executed plan: after the time and place of the
action have been sketched, the characters are
brought on to the scene or briefly described and
introduced. There then follows an hieratic or
even liturgical discussion on the secret of the
"mystery play", sometimes followed by a hymn
of praise and thanksgiving from the privileged
ones for God's redemptive intervention in the
history of mankind. This dialogue with its relevant hymn (if any) forms the nucleus, the central
part of every scene and concludes with the
observation that the actors are leaving the stage
or the scene of action. A list of the scenes in

Luke i–ii comprises the following items: the annunciation of the angel to Zechariah (i.5–25) and to Mary (i.26–38); the visitation of Mary to Elizabeth (i.39–56); the birth and circumcision of John the Baptist with its attendant incidents (i.57–80); the birth and circumcision of Jesus with its correlated events, including in particular the story of the shepherds (ii.1–21); Jesus' presentation (ii.22–38) and the finding in the temple (ii.41–50). Reading the biblical passages in question will enable us to verify quite easily whether, and to what extent the above plan, which is anything but rigid, can be traced in these scenes.

2. *Construction*

More striking even than the rather schematic construction of the individual scenes is the special way they have been arranged in the childhood story as a whole, classified in accordance with a definite plan and composed in a well-defined literary construction. What else could we expect from an author who, in his prologue, declares his intention "having followed all things closely for some time past, to write an *orderly* account." (Luke i.3.) Quite possibly this "orderliness" was already present, fully or partially, in the Semitic substratum of Luke i–ii; but, however this may be, Luke, whose intention we know from the foreword to his gospel, had the final hand in the definitive edition of these chapters. Where order reigns there is no place for capriciousness or chaos but only for cohesion and consistency; there we can expect a fine interplay of agreement, contrast and parallelism; there we shall find an orderly development of ideas, some parts being given extra weight and emphasis whilst others are less heavily stressed, have less light thrown upon them and are made to appear of secondary importance.

Even a superficial reading immediately betrays the author's obvious intention to paint a diptych of the Baptist and Jesus, or rather—to put it more accurately—a double diptych. In the first, the birth of the two infants is solemnly announced by the angel Gabriel, to Zechariah and to Mary respectively. In a second diptych he paints their birth and circumcision. Hence we can speak of the diptych of the annunciations (i.5–25: the annunciation of the birth of John to his father Zechariah; i.26–38: the annunciation of Jesus' birth to his mother Mary) and the diptych of the nativities (i.57–80: the nativity of the Baptist; ii.1–21: the nativity of Jesus). Later on we shall note the symmetry and the consistent painting "technique" of these diptychs, but first we must consider the place of the other scenes in the remarkable structure of Luke i–ii.

We can base this study on a few elements in the text which, for all their initial strangeness and scant appeal to Western thought and feelings, are all the more in keeping with the Semitic nature of the narrative and can therefore be held as objective criteria. In this artistic literary composi-

tion there are, in fact, three verses that recur by
way of chorus and obviously have a part to play
in the overall construction. These fairly constant
formulae could be called the literary "seams" of
the composition; they indicate the main joins of
this word-picture, mark the transition from one
panel to the next, and bind the whole into a closely
knitted composition. The first chorus (A) is that
of the "leave-taking" which occurs at the end of
most scenes, defining them but at the same time
joining the diptych of the annunciations to that
of the nativities.[23] The second type (B) is the
chorus of the "growing-up" which is characteristic
of the diptych of the nativities and its correlated
stories.[24] The third chorus (C) is that of the
"treasuring".[25] This is what the structure of Luke
i–ii looks like in outline:

1. DIPTYCH OF THE ANNUNCIATIONS

1. Annunciation to   i.5–25   chorus A—i.23
   Zechariah
2. Annunciation to   i.26–38 chorus A—i.38
   Mary

inset

The visitation of   i.39–56   chorus A—i.56
Mary to Elizabeth

2. DIPTYCH OF THE NATIVITIES

1. Nativity of John   i.57–80   chorus B—i.80
2. Nativity of Jesus ii.1–21   chorus C—ii.19
                                and chorus A—ii.20

inset

The presentation ii.22–38 chorus B—ii.40
of Jesus in the   and chorus A—ii.39
temple

closing piece

The finding of   ii.41–50 chorus A—ii.51
Jesus in the   and chorus C—ii.51
temple   and chorus B—ii.52

This summary clearly shows us the role of the recurring choruses: they are in the real sense of the term joins which define the various panels and bind the whole into an imposing many-panelled painting.

Another brief word about the panels referred to as "insets" in this summary. Not only do they have a well-defined place between and after the diptychs—thanks to the choruses—but they also relate to the subject-matter: the mystery (or its aspects) dealt with in the diptychs. They could be regarded as an extension of, and a commentary on, the diptych to which they belong.[26] Thus the narrative of Mary's visitation to Elizabeth clarifies several details of the preceding diptych: John's hallowing—predicted in the annunciation to Zechariah in the words: "He will be filled with the Holy Spirit, even from his mother's womb" (i.15) —comes true in the joyful leaping of the baby in Elizabeth's womb (i.41, 44); this also applies to Mary's faith, expressed in her "fiat" (i.38) and praised by Elizabeth (i.45). Moreover, as we shall see later, this inset brings into clear relief the tendency which is present in the first diptych: in this contact between the two chosen ones, in this meeting between Old and New Testament in an atmosphere of messianic joy, the old Elizabeth recognizes the superiority of her young kinswoman. The same can be said about the inset after the second diptych: it paints the manifestation of the newborn Messiah in the temple where the prophetic figures of Simeon and Anna, representatives of Israel's redemptive hope, recognize and salute the long-awaited Redeemer.

In many respects the closing piece (ii.41–50) is a repetition of the preceding inset (ii.22–38): both scenes take place in the temple; they start with an ascent to the temple (ii.22 and ii.42) and end with a return to Nazareth (ii.39 and ii.51); in both instances we have a manifestation of Jesus. The sword of Simeon's prophecy (ii.35) finds its first realization in Mary's fear and sorrow as she seeks her lost child. (ii.48.) This closing piece also gives the transition to Jesus' public life: he does not belong in the family circle at Nazareth, but in the house of his Father, and, by virtue of his vocation and his nature, he must attend to the things that concern him. (ii.49.)

3. *Significance of this construction*

There can be nothing fortuitous in the way the individual narratives have been bound into one great and beautiful composition. This construc-

tion must be based on a train of thought, on the
author's aim and purpose. He mentally classifies
the material at his disposal; some he lays aside,
some he weighs up, incorporates, transposes,
elaborates or emphasizes until the whole, whether
thumbnail sketch or lengthy narrative, harmon-
izes in accordance with his aims.

The first point to note is that Luke i–ii is built
on the figure seven, the sacred figure of the bible
to which Jews are particularly sensitive. Just as
great orators and preachers eagerly clung (or
cling?) to the famous three "points" and certain
dramatists adhere to the "law" of the five acts, so
Jews like to build a narrative on the rhythmic and
sacred figure seven.[27] But fortunately this construction is more than the mere expression of the Jews'
predilection for certain numbers or the revelation
of the literary adroitness of an ancient author, as
we shall see further on.

Passing reference has already been made on
p. 40 to the parallelism between the individual
panels of the two diptychs. This parallelism or
symmetry shows up less clearly in the diptych of
the nativities but it is all the more striking in the
diptych of the annunciations—as illustrated in the
following summary.

Annunciation to	*Annunciation to*
Zechariah (i.5–25)	*Mary* (i.26–38)
the Baptist's parents	Mary and Joseph
are introduced to us;	are introduced to us;

apparition of the angel;	entry of the angel;
Zechariah's confusion;	Mary's confusion;
"Do not be afraid";	"Do not be afraid";
annunciation of the nativity;	annunciation of the nativity;
"How shall I know this?";	"How can this be?";
the angels' reply;	the angel's reply;
sign) you will be unable to speak;	*sign*) behold your kinswoman;
Zechariah's silence;	Mary's faithful reply;
Zechariah's exit.	the angel's exit.

As early as 1908 Père Allo OP used this parallelism to refute Harnack's assumption that the verses in the annunciation to Mary expressing Jesus' virgin birth (Luke i.34) had never belonged to the original text but had been added at a later date by the Christian community.[28]

But this parallelism not only offers the advantage of rendering Harnack's assumption entirely improbable; behind this parallelism in the external literary form lies a contrast of content. The author seems intent on confronting and contrasting the person, he paints in their characteristic traits and qualities in the different panels of the two diptychs and their relevant insets; in such a way that the main figures in the first panel of both diptychs are obviously the lesser of the main figures of the second panel. This is true of John's parents *vis-à-vis* Mary but especially of the Baptist *vis-à-vis* Jesus. It is really the figure of Jesus that has most light thrown upon it in the whole of Luke i–ii. In both diptychs the first panel is really the preparation for the second. Besides, the parallel construction is finally broken "in favour of" Jesus and the events around him: in the end the scales which, as it were, retain their equilibrium up to and including the second diptych are tipped clearly towards Jesus, the main character of the childhood story. This literary construction illustrates what the Baptist is to say later on: "He who is mightier than I is coming, the thong of whose sandals I am not worthy to untie." (Luke iii.16.)[29]

The striking contrast in the setting of the annunciations quite naturally recalls the sharp contrast between the persons depicted. In the panel of the annunciation of John's nativity we find ourselves in the holy city of Jerusalem, in the temple, right by the veil that divides the Holy Place from the Holy of Holies; here Zechariah reaches the climax of his priestly life and offers incense on the golden incense altar whilst in the various outer courts the Jewish people join in prayer in the solemn act of its representative. The panel of the annunciation of Jesus' birth takes us far from Jerusalem to an unknown and insignificant little village, not worthy of a mention in the Old Testament, the subject of Nathanael's later remark: "Can anything good come out of Naza-

46

reth?" (John. 1.46.) We are no longer in Judea but in the distant and despised, half-pagan Galilee. (Cf. 1 Mach. v.15.) Here the privileged one is not a priest of God's ancient people but a young and unknown girl. And yet, the event depicted in this second panel of the diptych of the annunciations is of far greater significance. It gives a foretaste of one of the basic traits of the New Testament's redemptive economy: God performs his greatest wonders in what is, humanly speaking, of little moment, in darkness and in silence, in the insignificance of his creatures: *virtus Dei in infirmitate humana* (God's strength in human frailty).

Another interesting point is the contrast between John's parents and Mary. In Luke i.6 Zechariah and Elizabeth are described as people who keep strictly to the old Law; Mary is given the name "kecharitōmenē": object of God's choice and grace. In the end John is naturally conceived (i.23–4) but of barren parents, as i.7 emphasizes: "They [Zechariah and Elizabeth] had no child, because Elizabeth was barren, and both were advanced in years"; thus this conception and birth are entirely in line with the "spiritual" birth of the redemptive figures of the Old Testament (cf. Gal. iv.29), though in the diptych of the nativities it is the preparation for an infinitely more "spiritual" conception of Jesus by the virgin Mary (cf. Luke i.26–7, 35). Zechariah is reprimanded by the angel for his lack of faith and by way of punishment he is struck dumb:

> Behold, you will be silent and unable to speak until the day that these things come to pass, because you did not believe my words, which will be fulfilled in their time [i.20.]

Immediately after this vision this sign of punishment is observed by the people outside. (i.22.) Mary, however, gives the divine message the sublimest answer a human being can give—her firm belief in God's word:

> Behold, I am the handmaid of the Lord; let it be to me according to your word [i.38.]

and Elizabeth recognizes her superiority and praises her faith. (i.45.) This contrast is carried forward into the second diptych: John's birth is the occasion for rejoicing among the neighbours, i.e., among humans (i.58); at Jesus' birth it is the heavenly host that brings the good news of a great joy to all the people on earth (ii.9–10).

Stronger still is the contrast between the children John and Jesus. The etymological significance of their names bears this out; John means "Yahweh has had pity, has bent down with kindness [over Israel]"; Jesus stands for "Yahweh is saviour, brings about salvation". Of John it is said: "He will be great before the Lord, and he shall drink no wine nor strong drink" (i.15); his greatness is human and relative (cf. the addition of the comparative clause: "before the Lord", as also in Ecclus. xlviii.22; Gen. x.9), and based on foreign ways—abstention from certain beverages: an outward symbol of a higher reality—dedication to the Lord (cf. 1 Sam. i.11; Judges xiii.4–7) by a certain rite. Of Jesus it is said, in i.32: "He will be great, and will be called the Son of the Most High"; at first this seems hardly different from the text of i.15 but it is notable that in this passage "great" is used absolutely, without the addition of a comparative clause; and as the Old Testament reserves this usage for Yahweh,[30] there is at least a suggestion that Jesus' greatness is the greatness of God himself. The mission of the two figures is also given a different characterization: John's mission is prospective, preparatory, prophetic: "He will go before him in the spirit and power of Elijah, to make ready for the Lord a people prepared" (i.17; cf. i.76 and Mal. iii.1); Jesus' mission is the definitive mission of the eschatological, messianic king who will reign forever on the throne of David (i.32–3). John is the messenger, the herald, the forerunner of the Lord; Jesus is the Messiah, the Son of the Most High. The contrast between them is obvious, and we may well ask if this contrast is not taken to the extent of affirming or at least suggesting Jesus' divine transcendence. I shall revert to this question in the next chapter but want to point out right now that this suggestion is actually made in three passages: i.32 ("great" without a comparative clause); i.35 (the title "Son of God" in this very context) and i.17, 76. The latter passage shows that Jesus is identified with "the Lord"— a title (*Kyrios*) which in the Greek translation of the Hebrew Old Testament (the Septuagint) is normally used to indicate Yahweh.

4

The Leading Thought
of Luke 1–2

(1) As I have already mentioned, the unfolding
of the story brings along a gradual breakdown of
the striking parallelism or symmetry of Luke i–ii.
Neither text nor content of these chapters appear
to lend themselves entirely to being confined
within the rigid, symmetrical lines of the diptychs,
but break through them. This seems to indicate
that under the static structure of Luke i–ii there is
a dynamic element that tips the scales, which long
remained in equipoise, more and more towards
Jesus, the "weightiest" character in these narratives. It is this dynamic element that now demands
our special attention. This is what gives the story
a certain direction and urges it towards an event
in the future, towards something that responds
to Israel's tense expectation as expressed by some
of the figures of bygone ages. Luke ii.25 speaks
of Simeon, a man who "was righteous and devout,
looking for the consolation of Israel", and a little
further we read about the prophetess Anna who
was present when Jesus was presented in the
temple: "She gave thanks to God, and spoke of
him to all who were looking for the redemption

of Israel." (ii.38.) Repeatedly mention is made of a mysterious fulfilment of the words spoken by the Lord (cf. i.20, 45, 57; ii.6, 21–2, 39) or of the days being fulfilled. (Cf. i.23; ii.6, 21–2.) God's Spirit which, according to Luke's description in the Acts of the Apostles, urges the young church on right from her inception and guides her development from Jerusalem to Rome, is also active here in Jesus' childhood, and with divine dynamism moves everything and everybody towards a fulfilment. This movement can even be felt on the "material" plane: the characters in the narrative are forever on the move, never stop going from place to place, on occasion even "with haste". (Cf. i.39; ii.16.) What is the direction of this movement? There are many indications that its ultimate goal lies in the distant future, in the period of the public appearance of an adult Jesus and particularly in his death, resurrection and exaltation. It is in the risen and glorified Lord Jesus that the words of the message are fully realized:

> "The Lord God will give to him the throne of his father David, and he will reign over the house of Jacob for ever; and of his kingdom there will be no end." [i.32–3.]

The same goes for Simeon's prophecy:

> "This child is set for the fall and rising of many in Israel and for a sign that is spoken against." [ii.34–5.]

But there is also a more immediate end to this movement, a nearer though provisional, as yet incomplete, fulfilment of the tense expectations within the framework and the compass of the childhood story itself. This end term is reached at the presentation of Jesus, at the moment when he enters the temple. The pericope on Jesus' finding in the temple, which concludes the childhood story, again underlines this in a manner that lacks nothing for clarity: "Did you not know that I must be in my Father's house?" (ii.49.) When Jesus enters into his Father's house, Simeon, a man "righteous and devout, looking for the consolation of Israel", can sing his *Nunc dimittis*:

> Lord, now lettest thou thy servant depart in peace, according to thy word; for mine eyes have seen thy salvation which thou hast prepared in the presence of all peoples, a light for revelation to the Gentiles, and for glory to thy people Israel. [ii.29–32.]

That is where the expectations of Israel are fulfilled.

(2) Jesus' ascent to the temple is the leading thought of Luke i–ii; this movement is the dynamic element that gives dash and momentum to the whole narrative and breaks its symmetry. The question now is what significance the author attaches to Jesus' entry into the temple. An adequate reply to this question must be based on a careful consideration of a few Old-Testament

passages to which the author refers and are to be found in the books of Malachi and Daniel. This reference to the Old Testament is a normal procedure in Luke i–ii, as we shall see in more detail in the following chapter; the author is continually doing it, often in a way that is not immediately apparent to us and is on occasion hard for us to appreciate. I shall confine myself here to those Old-Testament passages that are of importance for an accurate understanding of the leading thought, adding a brief word about the contents of the book in question.

The Book of Malachi is the final one in the series of the twelve minor prophets—in the fairly general consensus of opinion among exegetes derived from an anonymous, unknown author who was active as one of the last Old-Testament prophets in the first half of the fifth century BC between 516 and 445. Later on the book was ascribed to one "Malachi" (the name means "my messenger") on account of Mal. iii.1.[31] After the rebuilding of the temple in 516 and the restoration of its services, there seems to have been a period of spiritual tepidness and slackness among the Jews in and around Jerusalem, attributable among other reasons to the disappointment and disillusionment of the people because the messianic era was not forthcoming. Faced with the problem of explaining why the messianic kingdom did not dawn, the anonymous prophet of the Book of Malachi blames this in the first place on the

neglect of the religious prescriptions on the part
of the priests (i.6–ii.9) who by their lack of the
right inward disposition and their sinful hearts
turn the sacrifices which they offer to Yahweh
into caricatures; and by taking partisan decisions
fall short in their task as teachers of the Law. He
criticizes, moreover, the bad conduct of the Jews
whom he reproaches for social injustice, oppres-
sion of the poor, divorce and mixed marriages.
(ii.10–16.) It is the fault of the people itself, in all
its ranks, that the messianic kingdom fails to
dawn. Furthermore, the prophet wants to restore
the shaken faith in Yahweh: the day of the Lord
will undoubtedly come (ii.17–iii.5; iii.13–21)
when evil-doers shall be punished and the
righteous receive their reward. (iii.13–21.) For
that awful day of the Lord one should make
preparation by a renewal of life. Then Yahweh
will show himself to those who seek him (iii.1),
to the just of Israel (iii.4); the *eschaton* will be
ushered in (iii.2, 17, 19, 21); it is the day of judgement (iii.5); Yahweh shall restore the priesthood
to its erstwhile sanctity; it is the day of the renewal of the offering pleasing to God as in the
days of old. (iii.3–4.) The prophet mentions not a
word about the coming of the Messiah but says
Yahweh himself will come to his temple, his
place, which at present is despised and im-
poverished. At his coming he will be preceded
by a mysterious messenger, a forerunner who will
prepare the way before him. (iii.1.) In the epilogue

(iii.22–4)—probably a later addition and at the same time intended as the conclusion of the collection of minor prophets—this messenger is identified with Elijah:

> Behold, I will send you Elijah the prophet before the great and terrible day of the Lord comes. And he will turn the hearts of fathers to their children and the hearts of children to their fathers. [iv.5–6.]

There is a strikingly clear link between Mal. iv.5–6 and Gabriel's words to Zechariah in Luke i.16–17:

> And he will turn many of the sons of Israel to the Lord their God, and he will go before him in the spirit and power of Elijah, to turn the hearts of the fathers to the children, and . . . to make ready for the Lord a people prepared.[32]

The mysterious messenger and forerunner who prepares the way for the Lord is, therefore, identified in the message of the angel Gabriel with John the Baptist whose mission is described in words that clearly refer to Mal. iv.5–6. The same can be noted in Zechariah's song of praise (Luke i.76):

> And you, child, will be called the prophet of the Most High; for you will go before the Lord to prepare his ways. [Cf. Mal. iii.1; iv.5.]

This identification of John with the new Elijah is one that we are familiar with from the gospels.

(Cf. Luke vii.27; Matt. xi.10; xvii.10.) But not
only is this illumination of the figure of the
Baptist with quotations from Malachi an important means of arriving at the significance the
author attaches to the Baptist and his mission; it
is also evidence of his view of Jesus and of the
significance of Jesus' presentation in the temple.
For this messenger—identified with the Baptist—
prepares the way for the coming of Yahweh himself to the temple. Cf. Mal. iii.1:

> Behold, I [Yahweh] send my messenger to
> prepare the way before me, and the Lord whom
> you seek will suddenly come to his temple...

If the author of Luke i–ii has these Malachi
passages in mind when describing the person and
the task of John, the forerunner of Jesus, it is
obvious that, when he describes Jesus' entry into
the temple, he is thinking of Yahweh's coming
to the temple which is mentioned in the context
of Malachi: in Jesus' entry into the temple (Luke
ii.22–38) he sees a fulfilment of the coming of
Yahweh into the temple announced by Malachi.
(Mal. iii.1.)[33]

In this connection the conception of the liturgy
for the Feast of the Purification on 2 February is
remarkable. On this feast, which is not really a
feast of Mary but a feast of Christ kept in Jerusalem as early as the fourth century and universally
observed since the sixth century, the mass liturgy
relates the message of Malachi to Jesus' presenta-

tion in the temple, respectively in the epistle and gospel of the day. What the epistle (Mal. iii.1–4) teaches about the coming of the Lord (Yahweh) into his temple, the gospel (Luke ii.22–32) depicts as its fulfilment in Jesus' entry into the temple.[34] The author of the childhood story seems to incline towards the conception of the ancient liturgy. Various little traits in his temple stories (and therefore also in that of the finding in the temple, which has been shown to be in many respects the repetition of the preceding temple scene) seem to confirm that he had the wider context of the Book of Malachi in mind. Jesus is manifested to the righteous of Israel, represented by Simeon and Anna (cf. Luke ii.25, 38) who meet him and greet the dawn of a new era. (ii.29–32, 38.) He is found in the temple by those who seek him. (Cf. the term "seeking" that recurs four times in Luke ii.44–49.) Furthermore, we are reminded that with Jesus' presence the day of judgement has come: he brings the "crisis" closer and places man before a choice; he is set for the fall and rising of many in Israel . . . that thoughts out of many hearts may be revealed. (ii.34–5.) It is also the day of the new, pure sacrifice that is pleasing to God. (ii.24.) In this light the oft-recurring expression in Luke i–ii "the days were fulfilled" acquires a full and very deep meaning: the fullness of time, the new messianic era has dawned with Jesus' entry into the temple; in Jesus, Yahweh the Lord comes into his temple and the *eschaton* is rung in.

There is a further link with this. In the last verse of his hymn, Simeon greets Jesus, who has just come into the temple, as the "glory to [his] people Israel". "Glory" (the Greek: *doxa*) is an indication or a description of Yahweh who intervenes to save his people and lives with them. In Exod. xxiv.16 we read that "the glory of the Lord settled on Mount Sinai" when the covenant was made. When Yahweh takes possession of the tent of meeting and wants to be present there among his people, it is said that "the glory of the Lord filled the tabernacle". (Exod. xl.34–5.) The same expression is used when Yahweh occupies the temple—the house Solomon built for him—to live among his people who have in the meantime become sedentary. (1 Kings viii.10–11; 2 Chron. v.14; vii.1–3.) The Prophets frequently announce a new and definite residence of the glory of the Lord on Mount Sinai, in the temple, and this residence will come about in the eschaton:

> When the Lord shall have washed away the filth of the daughters of Zion and cleansed the bloodstains of Jerusalem ... the Lord will create over the whole site of Mount Zion and over her assemblies a cloud ... for over all the glory there will be a canopy and a pavilion. [Isa. iv.4–5; cf. xxiv.23; lx.1ff; lxvi.18ff; Ezek. ix.3; xliii.1ff.]

It had been revealed to Simeon by the Holy Ghost that he should not see death before he had seen the Lord's Christ (Luke ii.26); and indeed, when this anointed one entered into the temple, his eyes did see the glory of Israel (cf. ii.30–32) and therefore he could pray: "Lord, now lettest thou thy servant depart in peace." (ii.29.) The residence of the glory of Yahweh promised by the Prophets, the saving and redeeming presence of Yahweh with his people in the *eschaton*, is given its first fulfilment—in the eyes of the author —the moment the temple is entered by Jesus whose name signifies: Yahweh grants salvation and redemption, "for he will save his people from their sins". (Matt. i.21.)

(3) Another Old Testament book the author of Luke i–ii had in mind is that of Daniel. In it a distinction should be made between a biographical part (i–vi) and an apocalyptic (vii–xii) followed by two appendices (xiii–xiv). In the first part the author acquaints his readers with the great personality of the wise Daniel who gains distinction at the court of Babylon as a seer to whom God has revealed the course of world history. He is persecuted but endures all tribulations, thanks to his faith in God and his wisdom which is to be given repeated recognition. As to the interpretation of dreams, he excels the wise men of the pagan court (Dan. ii and iv) after the example of Joseph in Egypt. (Gen. xli.) The author, himself a wise man, manages to put his ideals across in the form of a few edifying and captivating narratives for which he draws on the rich treasure of popular

tradition. His aim is to encourage his contemporaries in the heavy days of persecution and
pagan infiltration under King Antiochus (175–
163 BC). In the first part of his book he prepares
the reader for what the genial, wise hero of his
story has to say in the second part about the dark
ages around the said Antiochus and about the
coming Kingdom of God.

This second part belongs to the literary *genre*—
a strange one to modern readers—which goes by
the name of revelational or apocalyptic. It
flourished and attracted considerable interest from
the second century BC until the third century of
the Christian era, particularly in a number of so-
called Jewish apocryphal works. It is a very
characteristic *genre* with its own laws and its own
theology. The apocalyptic writer is deeply aware
of the wickedness of this world which is cursed by
ever-increasing sinfulness and is therefore moving
to its doom. But God has also created another
world, a new era which is already in existence in
heaven. When corruption is at its blackest, God
will intervene and allow the new era to dawn. By
means of various visions the apocalyptic writer
can look into that other world right now and
this enables him to announce to "the servants of
God" "the things that are to happen" in order
that they shall take courage and, despite these
times of need and persecution, remain hopeful of
the coming salvation. In common with later
prophets (cf. Ezek. xxx.3; xxxviii–xxxix; Joel

iii–iv; Zech. ix–xiv), this literary *genre* is constantly concerned with the eschaton, with "the day of the Lord". Attempts are made to calculate the moment of the eschatological event by means of signs, symbols and various complicated figure speculations. When the other world is opened to the seer in visions, he is overcome, his powers collapse and he fails to understand the pictures he sees. Then comes the so-called *angelus interpres* (the interpreting angel) who accompanies the seer and explains the vision to him. Apocalyptic authors speak to their contemporaries under cover of pseudonyms—a well-known literary fiction. They set to their visions the names of great figures from Israel's past such as Enoch, Moses, Abraham, Ezra, Solomon, Baruch, Isaiah and others. The great revelations concerning the coming *eschaton* are therefore ascribed to these famous men by the real authors, they make out they received them in their literary form, recorded and sealed them against the time of their fulfilment, which is the age in which the authors and their readers live. This famous name was the bait; its enchantment was the authors' guarantee of being read.

The Book of Daniel is the model of apocalyptic writings and has inspired the later works. Its author is convinced that the history of mankind is in decline; the four continents are in an ever-growing decadence which culminates in King Antiochus IV. Nevertheless, everything happens according to a divine plan: in this time of dire

need the end is near; God himself will intervene
and establish an everlasting kingdom of sanctity.
The future of the world is revealed to the readers
in obscure symbolism and various complicated
and mysterious visions. In the vision of the ram
and the he-goat (Dan. viii.1–27) and in the revelation concerning the seventy years (Dan. ix.1–27),
the angel Gabriel acts as "interpreting angel" and
gives the seer the explanation he needs (viii.15ff.;
ix.21). In the latter passages the author expresses,
through David, the anxious uncertainty regarding
the seventy years that must elapse, according to
the prophet Jeremiah, after the destruction of
Jerusalem in 587, before Yahweh will resume the
care of his people. (Cf. Jer. xxix.10ff.; xxv.11ff.)
After a penitential prayer, in which Daniel joins
with the people in confessing his guilt to Yahweh
and entreats him to show mercy (ix.4–19), Gabriel
comes to him at the time of the evening sacrifice
to "enrich him with understanding" of God's
secret decisions:

> Seventy weeks of years are decreed concerning
> your people and your holy city, to finish the
> transgression, to put an end to sin, and to atone
> for iniquity, to bring in everlasting righteous-
> ness, to seal [fulfil] both vision and prophet,
> and to anoint the Holy of Holies. [ix.21–4.]

The divergent exegetic interpretations show
that this expression is not very clear. What is
meant in this passage by "the Holy of Holies"?

Is it a holy object or a place consecrated to God
such as an altar or a temple, or is it a person, a
high-priest, for instance, or the Messiah? Many
exegetes recall the re-dedication of altar and
temple by Judas Maccabeus in 164 BC. (Cf. 1
Macc. iv.41ff.) Others share the opinion—probably a more accurate one—that what is meant is
the spiritual temple, the spiritual community of
the messianic era dedicated to God. The author
announces here the inauguration of God's kingdom, symbolized in Dan. vii.13ff. by the coming
of the Messiah; the author despairs of man's
worldly empires whose impetuous, progressive
degeneration has turned them into a power
opposed to God. He only expects salvation from
above; by Yahweh's special intervention, on his
"day" the enemies of the Chosen People are
judged and punished, and, as a pure gift from
heaven, God's kingdom and dominion are established on earth among his people. Then sins are
wiped out and everlasting justice and sanctity
established, characteristic of the coming era. (Dan.
ix.24; cf. Isa. iv.3ff.; xi.9.) We note, however, that
several ancient translations of this passage from
Daniel, among them the Greek Septuagint, think
the intervention of a person is indicated by the
expression Holy of Holies. (ix.24.) There are
reasons for assuming these interpretations to have
been fairly current among the Jews of those times.
The Vulgate gives to understand that this expression is a direct pointer to the Messiah and thus

reflects the fairly general opinion of the ancient exegetes.[35] It is therefore quite in order to ask whether the author of Luke i–ii also associates himself with this interpretation and there are, in fact, reasons for thinking that he does.[36] The very mention of Gabriel in Luke i.19, 26 as God's messenger who brings the joyful tidings to Zechariah and Mary, immediately puts us in mind of Daniel's visions. In any event, it is striking that as far as the canonical books are concerned, Gabriel is exclusively mentioned in Dan. vii–ix and Luke i. Moreover, in both Dan. ix.21 and Luke i.10 he appears towards the hour of the evening sacrifice. Daniel sees him approaching "at the time of the evening sacrifice" and Zechariah "at the hour of incense" while the people were praying outside. In both passages there is a connection between the subject's prayer and the message received. The same Gabriel who comes to "enrich him with understanding" of God's coming kingdom, assures Zechariah at the moment when the fullness of time has arrived, that his prayer has been answered and that his spouse will give him a child which will have to prepare the way for the coming Lord. (Luke i.13–17, 26.) Six months later (i.26) he brings the message of messianic joy to Mary: she will conceive and bear a child, to be called holy. (i.35.) The expression "to be called holy" used by Gabriel in this passage from the annunciation to Mary, recurs at the beginning of the pericope of the presentation in the temple:

> And when the time came for their purification according to the law of Moses, they brought him up to Jerusalem to present him to the Lord (as it is written in the law of the Lord, "Every male that opens the womb shall be called holy to the Lord"). [Luke ii.22–3.]

This precept of the law can be found in Exod. xiii.2, 12–13; but the wonder of it is that we look in vain there for the expression "to be called holy". The author of Luke i–ii seems to have deliberately added it as an echo of the words of Gabriel in i.35, and he then links them to the words of the same angel in Dan. ix.24: ". . . to anoint the Holy of Holies". In Luke's interpretation of this passage from Daniel, Jesus is this "holy" one, who deserves this name *par excellence* and is anointed at the moment of the presentation in the temple. He is the Lord's Christ as ii.26 expressly states:

> "And it had been revealed to him by the Holy Spirit that he should not see death before he had seen the Lord's Christ."[87]

Now that "his days are fulfilled" in the deepest sense of the term, now that the day of the Lord has dawned and the new era is rung in, the Holy One is anointed Messiah and King in the temple of Jerusalem.

Strange though this harking-back to certain Old Testament passages, as instanced by Mal. iii, Exod. xl.34–5 and Daniel, may strike us, the following chapter will show that this process has been given an even wider application in Luke i–ii and is indeed one of the characteristics of these most Old Testament-conscious of New Testament narratives.

5

The Literary Genre
of Luke 1–2

In his encyclical letter *Divino Afflante Spiritu* of 30 September, 1943, Pope Pius XII wrote that the Catholic exegete falls short in his task if he does not make a study of the literary styles in which the ancient oriental was wont to express his thoughts. This is indeed one of the important essentials for understanding books of any sort and applies just as much to sacred ones.

As far as the latter are concerned, this study raises a further difficulty of its own, in that these ancient oriental styles should not be determined by our Western, modern mentality and are not the exact counterpart of the literary styles of either Greco-Roman or the modern literatures. Scientific examination and an adequate knowledge of ancient Oriental literatures are therefore an urgent necessity for any exegete. All too often the term "literary *genre*" is used as a slogan, a fashionable word which amateurs imagine they can use as a master-key to the solution of any difficulties that may arise, particularly in the historical field. But this does not serve the cause of biblical exegesis. The principle of the literary *genre* is undoubtedly sound and accordingly recognized as such in several ecclesiastical documents; but the exegete may—indeed he should—be expected to make a serious scientific examination of both the ancient oriental literature and the biblical books and to apply the principle with discretion and care.

"Literary *genre*" is an untranslatable expression indicating the various groups into which the literary products of the human mind can be classified. Thus in our literature we have, among others, the work of scientific historiography, the chronicle, the historical novel, the novel, the folk tale, the legend and the fable.

(1) What is the literary *genre* of Luke i–ii? The stories related in these chapters are without a doubt basically historical. Liberal exegetes regard these narratives as edifying legends sprung from the pious fantasy of the first Christians and modelled on the sagas of Hellenistic gods and heroes. They refuse to accept the miraculous nature of the childhood story in general and of Jesus' virgin birth in particular. For them it is a foregone conclusion that any story about an event which did not follow the laws of nature as we know them must be denied all historical value. The stories about Jesus' virgin birth must, they say, be based on a myth which was later given a Christian look and slipped into the biblical evidence. Pagan mythology does indeed have many sagas about so-called "sacred marriages" between gods and earthly women, which pro-

duced sons of gods. Similarly some historical figures are said to have been the sons of a god and an earthly mother. Tradition has it that Plato was a son of Apollo who had approached his mother in the shape of a swan. In their view, Hellenistic Christendom did not want to feel inferior in these and similar divine sagas and this is why they started to honour Jesus as a divine son— an adoration that brought about the story of the virgin birth. This explanation is absolutely untenable, as Karl Schelkle and others have demonstrated.[38] These myths, and indeed mythology as a whole, were regarded as unhistorical by pagans and Christians alike; nor is it conceivable that Christians accepted such stories about Jesus as really historical whilst holding those about divine sons of pagans to be idle myths. Moreover, the attempt to regard this point as an Hellenistic-pagan importation clashes with the strongly Palestinian and Jewish-Christian character of Matthew and Luke's childhood stories. Besides, no seriously minded investigator can deny that the concept of God as well as the whole spirit of the pagan myths differs in essence from the concept of God and the spirit of the childhood story.

The tendency to explain the New Testament from contemporary Hellenistic literature has, however, gradually made way for the view that the New Testament should primarily be interpreted from the Old Testament. In connection with the childhood gospel, reference is made particularly to the nativity stories of Isaac, Samson and Samuel; the nativity stories of the Baptist and Jesus are regarded as free compositions based on these ancient themes, as the deposit of the faith of the first Christian generation, and accordingly to be appraised as theology, not as history. Be that as it may, it is almost impossible for the data of the virgin birth to be explained from the spiritual treasure of the Old Testament. Jewry has never expected the promised Messiah to come into the world by a fatherless birth. The text of Isa. vii.14 ("a young woman shall conceive and bear a son") is nowhere related by the Jews of those days to the Messiah, let alone to the Messiah's birth of a virgin.

Nor can the doctrine of the virgin birth ultimately be regarded as a product of ancient Christian, early church speculative dogmatic theology. It never formed part of the general preaching, no more than did the whole childhood story, and the relevant tradition remained limited to a small group of Christians; but it does not follow that it is a theological construction of later date. It is precisely in the Epistle to the Hebrews and in John's Gospel—both writings of New-Testament theologians whose deepest thoughts are about the person and the work of Jesus—that this dogma does not appear. With them Jesus' divine sonship is never made dependent of his miraculous conception and birth.

In his prologue Luke specifically states that he

wants to give history and not the legendary product of a pious, creative fantasy, and confides to us his plan, intention and method:

> Inasmuch as many have undertaken to compile a narrative of the things which have been accomplished among us, just as they were delivered to us by those who from the beginning were eyewitnesses and ministers of the word, it seemed good to me also, having followed all things closely for some time past, to write an orderly account for you, most excellent Theophilus, that you may know the truth concerning the things of which you have been informed. [i.1–4.]

What he says here of the whole gospel can be applied, *mutatis mutandis*, to all its parts. Besides, many of the details of the childhood story can have no purpose other than relating history. Luke's foreword gives evidence of a great respect for the events that have occurred, and have been subjected to a detailed examination and that right from the very beginning. Apparently, he has gathered as much information as possible and, like the other Evangelists before him, he places himself respectfully under the authority of the first eyewitnesses and preachers. As I mentioned on pp. 15–16, in the composition of his childhood story he has probably used written Hebrew documents which in turn go back, through witnesses, to certain events in the childhood of the Baptist and of Jesus. These witnesses must naturally be sought in their respective family circles. Thus his childhood stories appear to refer, though vaguely and implicitly, to a few of John and Jesus' relatives who witnessed the events; for instance to Mary "who kept all these things, pondering them in her heart". (ii.19, 51.) Similarly in the story of John's birth and circumcision reference is made to Elizabeth's neighbours and relatives:

> And all these things were talked about through all the hill country of Judea; and all who heard them laid them up in their hearts, saying, "What then will this child be?" [i.65–66.]

Cf. also i.58; ii.20, 38. These references could be compared with the way John's Gospel appeals to the evidence of the beloved disciple: John xiii.23; xviii.15; xix.26.[39]

Finally we should note that the parallels between Luke i–ii and Matthew's childhood story are a guarantee for the historical reliability of the central events. In view of the great differences between them, Matthew and Luke's childhood stories originate from two different traditions and must be regarded as two substantive and independent depositions. It is all the more important that both agree as to the decisive events: Mary is betrothed to Joseph, a descendant of David; Jesus is conceived of the Holy Ghost and born of the virgin Mary; the birth took place in Bethlehem, though Nazareth is their home town; Joseph is not Jesus' real father. We have therefore a two-fold testimony for the central events which can, accordingly, stand up to the test of historical criticism.

(2) Nevertheless it immediately strikes us that the author's treatment of these events differs entirely from that of, say, a modern, scientific historical manual. His is no continuous chronicle, no full report of the events; the author picks and chooses, restricts himself to the scenes enumerated in Chapter 3 of this book and sets them out according to a well-defined plan. There is an extreme vagueness, too, about the chronological details of Luke i–ii. The annunciation to Zechariah is dated "in the days of Herod, king of Judea" (i.5), that is between 37 and 4 BC; the annunciation to Mary (i.26) is chronologically just as vague: "in the sixth month" (after Elizabeth had conceived her child) and therefore shares the vagueness of the narrative of his first annunciation. The pericope about Mary's visitation to Elizabeth begins: "in those days...". (i.39.) The birth of Jesus in Bethlehem is linked with a registration held all over the world by order of the Emperor Augustus, when Quirinius was Governor of Syria (ii.1–2); but to date the experts have been unable to establish with any certainty the year in question. The further general observation can be made that there is very little in these chapters to satisfy our (more or less profane) curiosity and the

historian's thirst for knowledge. This is religious historiography biblically presented, with close leanings to more ancient bible stories, especially as regards the annunciation narratives. The author uses biblical settings and traditional layouts, particularly when human means of expression fail him.

Thus the many points of contact between certain visions from the Book of Daniel and the apparition of the angel to Zechariah and to Mary, show that the author is giving these passages an *apocalyptic setting*.[40] The very name of the angel who introduces himself to Zechariah in Luke i.19 with the words: "I am Gabriel", immediately calls to mind the visions from the Book of Daniel. Whilst Zechariah is busy in the temple, offering incense, "the whole multitude of the men were praying outside at the hour of incense". (Luke i.10.) No mention is made of whether Zechariah, too, is at prayer before the vision, although the vision is a reply to his prayer: "for your prayer is heard". (i.13.) Similarly, Daniel, in ix.21, says the angel appeared "while I was speaking in prayer". (Cf. ix.23.) The presence of the people in Luke i.10 indicates that this verse refers to the evening sacrifice, just as in Dan. ix.21 the apparition of the angel occurs "at the time of the evening sacrifice". In Luke i.12–13 we read:

And Zechariah was troubled when he saw him, and fear fell upon him. But the angel said to him, "Do not be afraid, Zechariah".

75

Daniel too is gripped by fear:

> So I was left alone and saw this great vision,
> and no strength was left in me; my radiant
> appearance was fearfully changed, and I re-
> tained no strength. Then I heard the sound of
> his words; and when I heard the sound of his
> words, I fell on my face in a deep sleep with
> my face to the ground. [x.8–9.]

Luke i.19 goes on: "I am Gabriel, who stands in
the presence of God; and I was sent to speak to
you"; the angel describes himself here in his two-
fold function as a Throne and a messenger, as in
Dan. x.11: "... give heed to the words that I
speak to you ... for now I have been sent to
you". In Dan. vii.16 the angel who gives an
explanation is "one of those who stood there (before God, the ancient of days)". According to
Luke i.20, Gabriel says: "Behold, you will be
silent and unable to speak ..."; of Daniel it is
said: "... and [I] was dumb and behold, one in
the likeness of the sons of men touched my lips;
then I opened my mouth and spoke ..." (x.15–
16); similarly in Luke i.64 we read that there
came an end to his silence: "his mouth was
opened ... and he spoke". Luke i.21ff. says that
"the people were waiting for Zechariah, and they
wondered ...; and when he came out, he could
not speak to them, and they perceived that he had
seen a vision in the temple." Therefore, while the

people were standing outside, Zechariah was the sole witness of the vision; cf. Dan. x.7:

> And I, Daniel, alone saw the vision, for the men who were with me did not see the vision, but a great trembling fell upon them. [Cf. also Paul's vision in Acts ix.7; xxii.9.]

The name given to this apparition, "optasia", is a relatively rare one, used for the apparition of the angel to the women on Easter morning (Luke xxiv.23) and for Paul's vision at Damascus (Acts xxvi.19.) In the Greek Theodontion translation it occurs six times in Dan. ix.10.

What we have here is therefore an apocalyptic vision and, accordingly, we can speak of "an apocalypse of Zechariah". The annunciation to Mary belongs to the same *genre*, although the parallels with Daniel are less obvious. Apart from the angel Gabriel, we can point to the title "favoured one" (i.28); Daniel is addressed as "greatly beloved" (ix.23; x.11, 19). After being addressed, Mary was troubled and "considered in her mind what sort of greeting this might be"; Daniel too "sought to understand it" after he had seen the vision.

A study of the content of the message, within this apocalyptic framework, leads to the discovery that both with Zechariah (i.13–17) and with Mary (i.31–3) the author maintains *the style and the layout of the annunciation narratives of the Old Testament*. When the bible announces a birth,

through an angel, it invariably follows a fixed
plan that recurs time and again, except for a few
deviations. (Cf. Gen. xvi.11–12; xvii.19–20;
Judges xiii.3–5, 7; Isa. vii.14–17.) It is found in its
purest form in the message to Hagar in Gen.
xvi.11–12:

> And the angel of the Lord said to her, "Behold
> you are with child, and shall bear a son; you
> shall call his name Ishmael; because the Lord
> has given heed to your affliction. He shall be a
> wild ass of a man, his hand against every man
> and every man's hand against him; and he
> shall dwell over against all his kinsmen."

These layouts nearly always comprise the same
elements: pregnancy and birth, the naming of the
child, and its future. In Luke's text also this layout is relatively complete, though a few details
command our special attention.

(i) *Pregnancy and birth.* The annunciation of
John's birth, addressed to the child's father, as in
Gen. xvii.19, does not mention the pregnancy.
But this is no reason for assuming that Elizabeth's
pregnancy has already begun at the time of the
vision. Luke i.24 says: "After these days his wife
Elizabeth conceived", and in the bible's objective
narrative style this can only mean that the barren
wife became pregnant after the vision. In the
announcement of pregnancy and birth, both Luke
i.13 (your wife Elizabeth will bear you a son) and
i.31 (do not be afraid, Mary . . . behold, you will

conceive in your womb and bear a son) announce
something that lies in the future. In view of the
parallel nativity stories in the Bible, particularly
1 Sam. i and Judges xiii, we must assume that this
future is not far distant but near: for the mothers
of Samuel and Samson, pregnancy appears to
commence immediately after the prophecy or the
message.

(ii) *The naming of the child* normally follows
the announcement of pregnancy and birth and
takes the form of an order, usually coupled with
an explanation of the choice of name. This
element is missing in Luke i.13 and i.31, at least
in the usual form, for we can perhaps detect an
assimilation of this element in the phrase "for
your prayer is heard" (i.13): the Hebrew equivalent of John means "God is gracious" and it is
probable that an assumed Hebrew original uses
a substantive noun from the same root *chanan*
for "prayer".

(iii) *The child's future.* Its description constantly exceeds the individual viewpoint in a
marked degree. Thus Ishmael (Gen. xvi.12) and
Isaac (Gen. xvii.20) predict the future of a whole
people and this prediction of the future is at the
same time a command and a mission. Luke
i.32–3 carefully elaborates this:

> He will be great, and will be called the Son of
> the Most High; and the Lord God will give
> him the throne of his father David, and he will

reign over the house of Jacob for ever; and of his kingdom there will be no end.

Jesus is predicted here as the royal Messiah who will reign forever on David's throne. In him Nathan's prophecy was fulfilled:

> I will raise up your offspring after you, who shall come forth from your body, and I will establish his kingdom ... I will establish the throne of his kingdom for ever. I will be his father, and he shall be my son ... your throne shall be established for ever. [2 Sam. vii.12–16.]

The expression "son of the Most High" in Luke i.32 is not, therefore, an affirmation of Jesus' divine nature, but rather a messianic title. (Cf. Luke iv.41; Acts ix.20.) In i.16–17 John is described as the new Elijah, the eschatological prophet, and the wording used is borrowed from the familiar passages from the Book of Malachi. (Cf. pp. 61ff.)

Apart from the style and the layout of the biblical annunciation *genre* we come across a few elements in Luke i that are characteristic of and peculiar to *the fixed layout of the narratives of Old Testament calls* with their frequent repetition of the same development: Yahweh's call and mission—objection by the person called—the objection overruled by a promise—a sign in confirmation of the promise given or only requested. Let us compare one or two of these biblical calls.

The call of Gideon in Judges vi

(a) Order from Yahweh to Gabriel: I send you to liberate Israel. (vi.14.)

(b) Gideon's objection: I am too insignificant. (vi.15.)

(c) Refutation of the objection with a promise: I shall be with you. (vi.16.)

(d) The sign requested by Gideon. (vi.17–18.)

The call of Moses in Exod. iii

(a) Order to Moses: Go to Pharoah to lead the Israelites out of Egypt. (iii.10.)

(b) Objection from Moses: Who am I. . . .? (iii.11.)

(c) Refutation of the objection raised with the promise: I am with you. (iii.12.)

(d) The sign sent in confirmation by Yahweh: You shall adore God on this mountain. (iii.12.)

The call of Jeremiah in Jer. i

(a) The call to be a prophet. (i.5.)

(b) Objection of Jeremiah: I cannot speak and am too young. (i.6.)

(c) Refutation of the objection with the promise: I am with you. (i.7–8.)

(d) The sign to show that Yahweh puts the words in his mouth: the symbolic touching of the mouth. (i.9–10.)

We observe that in the narrative of each call there is a stereotyped recurrence of the request for a sign. This sign does not serve as an authentication of the apparition but as a confirmation of the mission. The Old Testament sees nothing reprehensible in the request for such a sign; it is not just a proof or an expression of disbelief (cf. Gen. xv.8; Isa. vii.13) and it is frequently given by Yahweh or his prophet.

These data are especially valuable for explaining the apparitions in Luke i which closely follow the pattern of the call narrative. After the message, containing Yahweh's selection of the person called (i.13–17 and i.30–33) there comes Zechariah and Mary's objection (i.18 and i.34); then the refutation of the objection by the angel (i.19 and i.35) and the requested sign (i.20 and i.36). Zechariah's objection to the content of the message is his wife's advanced age as well as his own, and he asks: "How shall I know this?" Mary is called to become the mother of the Messiah, in the near future—in line with the nativity annunciations in the Old Testament. But since she has no relations with a man and is only a betrothed girl, she offers the objection: "How can this be, since I have no husband?" The term "how" in this context does not mean "in what way"; in fact it indicates an impossibility: "But this cannot be in my present situation." Her question therefore boils down to a request for a sign, since the message appears an impossible one to her. In his reply the angel confirms that message: by God's special intervention she will become the Messiah's virgin mother. After this confirmation, the angel announces the sign: Elizabeth's pregnancy. Mary immediately notices the sign: "The babe leaped in her womb." (i.41, 44.) With Zechariah we find a similar request for a sign; it is given to him in his dumbness (i.20) and immediately after the vision the sign is observed by the crowd waiting outside. (i.22.) Nevertheless, we are confronted with an unexpected surprise: the dumbness is a sign of punishment, because he has not believed. It is not clear why the father of the prophet is described as an unbeliever though it is possible that the antithetic parallelism between John and Jesus and between Zechariah and Mary, which I have closely examined on p. 46ff., was the decisive factor: Zechariah is punished for his unbelief whereas Mary is called blessed because of her faith. (i.45.)

Having distinguished in Luke's annunciation stories the specifically apocalyptic setting and the pattern of the Old-Testament narratives of annunciation and call, honesty compels me to admit that to a certain extent this is but literary form. It is hard to believe that the divine messenger himself was bound to a definite plan; it is the human author who uses these traditional, biblical, features. Nor is there anything remarkable in it. We know from the Synoptic Gospels, and still more from the fourth gospel, that the authors allow themselves fairly considerable liberties, even when an accurate reproduction of words and facts is possible and indeed expected, for instance in the reproduction of the words of the consecration. All the more reason for expecting such a free rendering where it concerns "words which man may not utter". (2 Cor. xii.4.) The concrete form of the story must be put down to the narrator, who writes according to his religious views.[41]

(3) It will be clear from the foregoing that various texts, formulas, words and details of Luke i–ii are inspired by passages from the Old Testament. R. Laurentin (pp. 93ff.) sees such a process as a pointer to a literary *genre* which is known by expert exegetes as *midrash*. Before taking a closer look at the *midrash* character of Luke i–ii, a brief word about the significance and the origin of the midrash type in general.

The term *midrash*, derived from the Hebrew verb *darash* (to seek, examine), means "examination", "study", "meditation". Generally speaking, the subject of such an examination or meditation are Yahweh's mighty deeds, his intervention in Israel's history (Ps. cxi.2: "Great are the works of the Lord, studied by all who have pleasure in them") or the Law, the whole of God's revelation contained in Scripture. (Cf. Ps. cxix.) Ecclus. li.23 speaks of the *midrash*-house or the place where the Scriptures were attentively studied, meditated and explained in a way that was conducive to the teaching and edification of the people. The origin of this examination of the Scriptures must probably be sought in the exilic period, when the people were done out of land, temple and monarchy and the Sacred Books were their sole stay. During these years of trial, their thoughts turned to Yahweh's intervention in the past, his faithfulness to his chosen people and the people's unfaithfulness to him. The religious inheritance of the Fathers was pondered and among the people there developed a nucleus which came to religious fruition, repented and regained a deep awareness of Israel's true calling and destiny. Those were years of retreat and meditation, when the old traditions of Moses and the Prophets' sermons were read again and again, when ancient texts were searched for insight and solace in the entirely different situation then obtaining and for a programme for the future. After the return from exile this religious nucleus groups itself around Jerusalem and concentrates, under the guidance of the priests, on the altar and the religious observance in the restored temple and on the Sacred Books. Within this Jewish community in and around the holy city the greater part of the Old-Testament books are given the form we now know. The Law becomes the authoritative norm for the detailed regulation of community life. The ancient sacred texts are read, meditated, preached, studied, prayed and applied to the present situation.

The priests, who wield considerable authority, are the people's official teachers and religious

leaders, sought out for interpretation of the Law.
(Cf. Hag. ii.11; Mal. ii.7; Ezek. xliv.15, 24.)
Gradually there springs up within and alongside
the priestly circles the class of the *sopherim* or
scribes, who study and explain the Law—the first
of the so-called "men learned in Scripture", who
have so great an authority in Jesus' time. As we
see, various groups come about who in constant
study and meditation make the Old Testament
their spiritual sustenance and share this food with
the people entrusted to their leadership. They
develop an enormous activity which is deposited
in an extensive literature: homilies, sermons,
scriptural interpretations, instructions, edifying
stories etc. Again and again reference is made to
the older biblical books and actual problems are
treated in the light of the ancient texts. The post-
exilic books are often dependent on older biblical
books to which they refer explicitly and implicitly,
in free or verbatim quotations and allusions—a
frequent occurrence, often accompanied by deli-
cate word-play. Thus in Ecclus. xliv–1 we find a
series of portraits of great figures from redemptive
history in a meditative text which is really a fine
wove of ancient scriptural quotations and allusions. All sorts of words, expressions, motifs,
and the like from older books are repeated, not as
an exact, literal reproduction, but as a more
elaborate version of the original message, applied,
developed and transposed in accordance with a
deeper understanding of the revelational stage

actually reached, and related to the present times. The basis of this process is the conviction that Scripture contains God's living Word which speaks to his people in a given time and situation but is also farther reaching: it speaks just as much to the people of all ages and gives meaning to new situations as well as a religious view on new problems.

A few further observations need to be added. If the meditation or reflection concerns a practical problem it is called a *halachic midrash*: ancient legislative passages are examined and studied with a view to deriving from those ancient laws a rule of conduct or a new direction for an actual situation. Instances can be found in Matt. xix.5; 1 Cor. v.13 and ix.9 which refer respectively to Gen. ii.24; Deut. xix.9 and xxv.4. Next to it there is the *haggadic midrash*, when a study and meditation is made of the narrative parts of the Sacred Books in order to grasp the religious meaning of God's intervention in Israel's history. An important, actual happening is then illuminated and clarified by means of those ancient bible stories in order to establish at the same time the religious significance of the present-day event. Both have had a considerable development in the later rabbinical literature, in which they frequently adopt very subtle forms and are often overgrown with all kinds of legendary data—the result of an unbridled imagination. Thus the term *midrash* became congenitally contaminated and the *midrash* literature got a bad reputation with many scholars and became synonymous with fable or legend. But it was not like that right from the beginning.[42] Nor do we come across such excesses in the Scripture passages or books which have a *midrash* character, even though the comparatively great freedom with which ancient texts are again used and interpreted mislead a modern reader. Finally, such a *midrash* can take the form of a commentary, either explaining verse by verse or inserting all kinds of brief or lengthy glosses in the text, such as, for instance, the commentary on the Book of Habakkuk from the monastery at Qumran near the Dead Sea; or, as often happens, it can be an entirely new work, built up as a new edifice from the second-hand stones of earlier bible texts. (e.g. Ps. li and lxxii.)

The author of the childhood story reverts to the *midrash* type, familiar to his readers; naturally a *midrash* of the *haggadic* type. What he gives is not a reporter's story, no eyewitness report of what took place in Nazareth and Bethlehem at the incarnation and birth of Jesus. He narrates facts, certainly, but he does not describe in detail how, when, where and at what time the events occurred. He is no reporter who wants to bring a wealth of detail to the reader's notice and to repeat verbatim what was said. He does not narrate the events with the accuracy of a police report. For that matter, this exactness was hardly important in preaching the message of the re-

demption. This is the work of an historian intent
on preaching and giving a theological exposition,
having first religiously meditated upon the significance of the events at Nazareth, Bethlehem and
Jerusalem. Apart from facts he also gives the
significance, explains the meaning of the event
within the framework of redemptive history; as
he tells his story, he clarifies and interprets his
narrative. And this Christian explanation, elucidation, and interpretation of the events around the
incarnation, birth and childhood of Jesus (and of
his forerunner) the sacred author achieves by constant reference to the Old Testament. He narrates
and describes the actual event of incarnation, birth
and childhood of Jesus (and of his forerunner)
in the light of earlier events in Israel's redemptive history and in words borrowed from the
major Prophets who so often and so variedly
announced the messianic future. This is what
gives these narratives about the childhood of John
and Jesus such a strongly Semitic and Old-Testament character. If at first the text seems almost
idyllic, a closer look shows it to be interspersed
with Old-Testament reminiscences, comparable
to the preaching technique of St Bernard or
Newman who are also given to interpreting New-
Testament details by means of Old-Testament
thoughts and words.

There now follows a survey of the main
passages which, according to R. Laurentin and
several other exegetes, Luke alludes to and assimi-

lates in his meditative description. The disadvantage of this method—a partial repetition—is counteracted by the grouping of all the relevant material in one spot.

S. Lyonnet[43] points to the strong resemblance between the nativity stories of Samson (Judges xiii) and Samuel (1 Sam. i–ii) and the annunciation of John's birth. Luke has been inspired by these ancient bible stories, and he borrows certain expressions from them because they happened to be the obvious way of describing the birth and childhood of important figures from redemptive history. Luke paints the Baptist as the last of a line of children of quasi-virgin birth of a barren mother and thus, in an altogether special way, of divine parentage, like Isaac (cf. Luke i.37 and Gen. xviii.14) and Joseph (cf. Luke i.25 and Gen. xxx.22). All these characters are prefigurations of him who was born of the virgin Mary and in a very special way the son of God. By means of these reminiscences the author gives his narrative a biblical stamp and brings out that the births of John and, particularly, of Jesus are an extension of God's redemptive actions in the past and even their consummation. Both are heirs to the great figures from the Old Testament. Before reaching its climax and fulfilment in the Messiah, the history of Israel is, as it were, condensed and embodied in the Forerunner.

J. Audet[44] has made a special study of the *genre* of the annunciation stories. He draws attention to the strong relationship between the story of the annunciation of Mary (Luke i.26–38) and the message to Gideon (Judges vi.11–24). Gideon receives a new name ("brave hero") from the angel to characterize his future mission. The new name which the angel gives to Mary is *kecharitomene*, to be translated, according to Audet, as "chosen one" or "privileged one"; Mary is the one of whom the Prophets have spoken. Hence her confusion and her question: "How can this be?"[45]

P. Benoit[46] points especially to the parallels with the nativity stories of Isaac (Gen. xviii.11 = Luke i.7; Gen. xvii.19 = Luke i.13; Gen. xv.8 = Luke i.18; Gen. xxi.6 = Luke i.58), Jacob (Gen. xxv.24 = Luke i.57) and Joseph (Gen. xxx.23 = Luke i.25). Some elements and motifs from these narratives have apparently served as models for the heavenly annunciation of John's miraculous birth under the guarantee of a sign.

In imitation of R. Laurentin I have already indicated in the previous chapter the contact between Luke on the one hand and the books of Daniel and Malachi on the other. The name as well as the mission of Gabriel, who appears at the time of the evening sacrifice, allude, among other passages, to Dan. ix.21ff.

According to R. Laurentin[47] the prophecy of the weeks of years in Dan. ix and the messianic prediction in Mal. iii are the points of focus. Both predict the solemn entry of the Messiah into the temple, and these prophecies find their fulfilment in the presentation in the temple. This author goes on to indicate many other biblical passages used by Luke to illuminate and explain the actual happening he has pondered in pious meditation: Isa. viii.23–ix.6 (cf. Luke i.26, 32); Isa. vii.14 (cf. Luke i.27, 31); Zeph. iii.14–17 and the parallel texts Joel ii.21–7; Zech. ix.9–10 (cf. Luke i.28, 30); 2 Sam. vii.12–16 (cf. Luke i.32–3); Isa. xi.2 (cf. Luke i.35); Exod. xl.34–5 (cf. Luke i.35; also Num. ix.18, 22; 2 Chron. v.7; vi.2); Gen. xviii.14 (cf. Luke i.37). According to him the story of Mary's visitation to Elizabeth is in many ways a reminder of the story of the translation of the Ark by David to Jerusalem, described in 2 Sam. vi.2–11. Luke i.42 recalls Judith xiii.18–19. In Luke ii.1–14 he sees an allusion to Mic. iv.7–v.5.

He goes on to compare Luke ii.35 (the sword that pierces Mary) with Ezek. xiv.17 and Luke ii.34 with Isa. viii.14. The *Magnificat* he regards as an anthology from various Old-Testament passages, many ancient biblical texts being assimilated into a new composition. Similar observations can be made regarding the hymn of Zechariah (i.68–79) and that of Simeon (ii.29–32).

This imposing list composed by Laurentin and others proves that a considerable part of the edifice of Luke i–ii can, without exaggeration, be said to have been constructed with a certain measure of refinement from Old-Testament stones. It would be particularly instructive to take the trouble to read and carefully compare the passages quoted. It might very likely lead to the disappointing observation that no links can be found between the passages from Luke and the ancient biblical texts—or only very faint ones. Indeed these links are not equally and universally clear and strong; sometimes they are subtle and obscure and can even seem laboured in the eyes of one who does not feel at home in the Old Testament. He should, above all, reflect that this difficulty is greatly reduced and even removed if considered on the plane of an author who is thoroughly imbued with the bible. Such a sacred author, and certainly the author of his sources has, through the reading of the Scriptures followed by interpretation and sermons (in *midrash* form) in synagogal worship, grown familiar with the sacred narratives and with the formulas, themes and motifs which keep cropping up in the Old Testament. He thinks and speaks spontaneously in scriptural reminiscences; he can play with them and indeed does so, with the playfulness of the Jewish mind, so that the western bible reader of today may get the impression that the story is concerned with lighthearted pleasantries. Another point to bear in mind is that any comparison should be made between the Greek translation of the Old Testament and Luke's Greek text. Indeed, in any translation it can easily happen that the similarity between texts grows fainter or even disappears, for instance, because the same Greek

93

word is not translated by one and the same term. A final observation: There is practically no mechanical, literal, copying of the Old-Testament texts; the author is not guilty of rough material plagiarism of the Old Testament. With his data on the birth and childhood of John and Jesus as his starting-point, he searches the Old Testament for models, formulas and motifs with which to form and shape his narrative and give his details a religious interpretation. He uses, mixes and combines all these familiar biblical colours on his palette in a workmanlike fashion in order to paint a few diptychs which are both traditional and original, making the biblical colouring serve the Christian meaning of the data.

It can be most instructive to compare Luke and Matthew's childhood stories from the point of view of the use they make of the Old Testament. Matthew, too, makes references to the Old Testament, but his are explicit, systematic and decidedly apologetic: the stories in the first two chapters of his gospel repeatedly culminate or end in an Old-Testament prophecy, quoted explicitly to show that Jesus is the Messiah announced by the prophets; cf. Matt. i.23; ii.6, 15, 18, 23. Luke is implicit, except in ii.22–4, and much more discreet: he assimilates the Old Testament in the description itself. All sorts of Old-Testament terms and formulas run through his narrative like a golden thread. The Old and the New Testament intermingle in these chapters which lie at the intersection of both Testaments: the New-Testament data are interpreted in Old-Testament words. This is why the use of the Old Testament in Luke's childhood stories is less obvious than it is in Matthew's, who is explicit and therefore clearer.

This process raises obvious queries as to the historical value of these narratives. Could not the conclusion be drawn from Luke's literary play, which I have depicted above, or from his sources, that what we have here is not history but a purely literary construction?

In answer to this obvious question it should be noted that it is definitely going too far to treat the whole of Luke's childhood story alike.[48] Another reading of the passages in question will show that most parallel passages occur in both annunciations, in the story of the shepherds and in the hymns (*Magnificat*, *Benedictus* and *Nunc dimittis*). In Chapter 3, I observed that particularly the annunciations have a strong symmetrical construction; for the rest, the narratives run a more individual course, though within the framework of the familiar parallelism between the stories of John and those of Jesus. This is an indication that we are not dealing with a universally identical construction and that the *midrash* character is not everywhere equally strong. The author was apparently not in possession of accurate details in respect of certain events, especially the annunciations, partly, no doubt, because of the nature of the incidents, he was therefore compelled to bolster up his narrative in those places, and the ancient, traditional, biblical material stood him in good stead. For other parts of his narrative he seems to have had more concrete details so that the symmetrical construction and the *midrash genre* returns more pronouncedly and the historical quality increases, though even here the event and its Christian interpretation are interwoven in the narrative. The authors of the New Testament writings do not set out to give a report of the events but rather a religious view of the historic event which, so far from obscuring it, can give it a clearer and loftier meaning.[49]

The heart of the narrative of Luke i–ii, at least in so far as the stories about Jesus are concerned, probably goes back to Mary, the chief witness and of many events the only one. She has pondered her experiences in the light of Old-Testament characters and passages, and in her contemplative mind these reminiscences have perhaps partly acquired their initial typical form. The Greek word for "contemplate" which occurs in Luke ii.19 can also be translated as "compare": her experiences and the mighty deeds which God did to her she compared in her meditations with what he had previously done and said in the *praeparatio evangelica*, in Israel's redemptive history. The author of Luke i–ii who is convinced that Jesus' coming has been prepared by God and forms the cornerstone, the crowning and fulfilment of the promises made to Abraham and of the prophecies, has in any event elaborated and developed his details in this spirit. The final result of this religious, contemplative elucidation of the new data by means of God's preparatory activities and words in the Old Testament is what we find in our text of Luke i–ii.

6

The Meaning of the Events and the Significance of the Characters in Luke I–2

HAVING said all this, I must make the point that the events narrated in these contemplative stories of Luke i–ii are so interwoven and intermingled with the relevant explanatory Old-Testament quotations that it is difficult, if not impossible, to separate them and to distinguish where the "objective" facts end and their explanation and illumination by means of the Old Testament begins. Both are fused into one harmonious entity. In these joyful, melodious chapters the events have an harmonious accompaniment of Old-Testament sounds and tunes which, no doubt, had a familiar ring in the ears of the author and of the first Christians, and even now gives the whole composition the air of a beautiful polyphonic song, at least for those who can appreciate the Old-Testament accompaniment.

In consequence, some of the queries raised on these narratives from very human and understandable, and maybe even more or less profane, curiosity, are really irrelevant. Questions such as "What exactly took place?" assume this to be a detailed statement or a newspaper report and, however strange it may seem, they are not in order, nor are they in keeping with the literary *genre* of Luke i–ii. They may be asked, of course, but it should cause neither astonishment nor disappointment if they fail to elicit a reply, or only a lame one. It would be more to the point and more profitable to question the religious content of these stories.

The constant allusion to the Old Testament in this treatment of New-Testament events constitutes an enrichment of the Old Testament: the details of Old-Testament revelations are illuminated by the fullness of time and thus reach a loftier fulfilment. But this process also means an enrichment and deepening of New-Testament facts like the incarnation, birth and childhood of Jesus, Mary's motherhood and Jesus' ascent to the temple, and others. Thus the events acquire their Christian meaning. The harmonious Old-Testament accompaniment plays the same role and has the same effect as the perspective that gives a painting its depth. For those who can understand this accompaniment the narrative acquires greater depth and background; the figures in these stories are placed in special relief and gain an extra dimension. It may well be that there is thus less occasion for sentimentality or for a kind of religious romanticism but it does enable us to penetrate right down to an authentic, early Christian piety which will no doubt also appeal to modern man.

The main figure of Luke i–ii is without question Jesus. Compared with him all the other characters are of secondary importance and occupy a subordinate position: Elizabeth, Zechariah, Simeon, Ann, the shepherds and also John and Mary. The latter two, however, have a special relation with the main character, Jesus: the former as his forerunner and herald, the latter as his mother. The significance accorded by the author in this perspective to the person of Jesus has already been indicated to some extent when I spoke about the leading thought of Luke i–ii. The person of John has also been discussed several times. In this final chapter I shall pay particular attention to the figure of Mary. Against what background does the author see her? What significance does the author of the childhood story attach to this woman who, as mother, is inseparably linked with her son Jesus? We shall see that the author identifies her in turn as the Ark of the Covenant and as the daughter of Zion.

1. *Mary, the Ark of the New Covenant*

The story of the annunciation of Mary is divided into two parts by the question she raises in i.34: "How can this be, since I have no husband?" Luke goes on:

And the angel said to her, "The Holy Spirit will come upon you, and the power of the Most High will overshadow you; therefore the child to be born will be called holy, the Son of God." [i.35.]

The expression "Holy Spirit" should be understood in the Old-Testament sense of "the Spirit of the Lord God" and accordingly means the Lord God himself who is actively present with his people and in that people brings his work to completion. The Prophets speak of a special activity of the Lord's Spirit in the messianic era. (Isa. xi.11–16; lxi.1–3: Ezek. xxxvi.25–8; Jer. xxxi.31–3.) Moreover, in i.35 the term "Spirit of the Lord", in truly characteristic Semitic style, runs parallel with "the power of the Most High" —another indication of Yahweh himself; but this parallel passage also defines the sense in which Yahweh will be actively present with Mary or, as the text has it, come upon her. He will overshadow her or, in the literal translation of the Greek verb, "cover her with his shadow"—an expression that takes us back to a series of highly characteristic Old-Testament passages.

Thus, at the end of the Book of Exodus the author speaks of the building of Yahweh's house (the tent); and when all the work is completed he describes how Yahweh takes possession of this house or tent:

Then the cloud covered the tent of the meeting, and the glory of the Lord filled the tabernacle. And Moses was not able to enter the tent of meeting, because the cloud *abode upon it*, and the glory of the Lord filled the tabernacle. [Exod. xl.34–5.]

To understand this passage one must realize that the term "cloud" is a favourite expression to indicate the shrouded, veiled presence of Yahweh among his people. (Cf. Exod. xv.10; xix.9; Luke ix.34–5 and parallel passages.) "To cover with his shadow" is a characteristic expression to indicate Yahweh's residence in the midst of his people, in this case the tabernacle of the Covenant among the tents of the nomadic people. In the Book of Numbers we come across the same expression "overshadowing cloud", describing how God led his people through the desert:

"As long as the cloud rested over the tabernacle, they [the Israelites] remained in camp." [Num. ix.18, 22.]

When, after much wandering, the people finally settle in the promised land and take up residence in houses, Solomon also builds a house for Yahweh, the temple of Jerusalem. And when the Book of Chronicles describes how Yahweh takes possession of this house, the same thoughts emerge that were evident in connection with the occupation of the tent. (Cf. 2 Chron. v.7–vi.2.)

Now that his people have become sedentary, Yahweh lives among them in his house or, to put it more accurately, in the Holy of Holies, the holiest place in the temple. There he is enthroned above the cherubim on the ark which is his seat.

Yahweh's mysterious but real presence with his people, first in the tent and later in the temple, now becomes a presence in Mary, and Luke paints the Old Testament background by using the same expression *overshadowing* in the story of the annunciation of Mary. He obviously sees her as Yahweh's new house, as the ark of the New Covenant. Her womb is as a living Holy of Holies, where God takes up his abode at this important moment which sees the dawn of the messianic era. "Therefore", he continues, "the child to be born will be called holy". (i.35.) In the Litany of the blessed Virgin, Mary is invoked as the "ark of the Covenant", one of many biblical titles. The above exposition shows that Luke already saw her as the ark of the Covenant; which accounts for the view of many exegetes that the Virgin's messianic motherhood must also be regarded as a divine motherhood.

The deep significance of this identification within the framework of the childhood story can perhaps be clarified even further. According to Lyonnet and Burrows[50] Luke carries this identification right through into the story of Mary's visitation to Elizabeth (i.39–44, 56), immediately after the story of the annunciation, to which it is a kind of commentary. In this story of Mary's visitation he appears to be alluding to an Old-Testament pericope which describes the transfer of the ark by David to Jerusalem. (2 Sam. vi.2–19.) Both narratives speak of a journey in the land of Juda; just as the people of Jerusalem rejoiced at the arrival of the ark in the city, so Elizabeth rejoices when she is greeted by Mary, the ark of the new Covenant; just as David precedes the ark, dancing and leaping, so Elizabeth's child leaps for joy in his mother's womb. Compare also David's words: "How can *the ark of the Lord* come to me?" (2 Sam. vi.9) with Elizabeth's exclamation: "Why is this granted me, that *the mother of my Lord* should come to me?" (Luke i.43). Remember also that both 2 Sam. vi and Luke i–ii mention a journey to Jerusalem. (Cf. what has been said about the leading thought of Luke i–ii.) After the incident in which Uzzah is struck by God's hand for touching the ark and drops dead, David grows afraid of this awful God; he refuses to take the ark to the city of David and shelters it in the house of Obededom where it remains for three months. But when he sees that Yahweh blesses the house and its occupants, he does take it to the holy city. The great leading thought of Luke i–ii is Jesus' ascent to the temple of Jerusalem—his destination, the place where he must be. He is taken there by Mary who carries him as his mother, just as in the old redemptive economy the ark was the carrier and the throne of Yahweh. In this journey of Jesus (= Yahweh saves) to the temple of Jerusalem, the stay of "about three months" that Mary, the ark of the new Covenant, makes in the house of Elizabeth and Zechariah is no more than an interlude; and here too God's presence in Mary, the new ark, is a source of especial blessing on the house and on those who dwell in it. (Cf. i.41, 44.)

2. Mary, daughter of Zion

To explain this strange title "daughter of Zion", I must refer briefly to the familiar Old-Testament picture of marriage which is often used, especially in prophetic literature, to indicate the relationship between Yahweh and his people.

Between Yahweh and his chosen people there exists the same intimate relationship as that between husband and wife in marriage. Yahweh is the bridegroom who seeks his bride, the people of Israel, and procures her release from Egypt, the house of bondage. The marriage between the two partners is solemnized on Mount Sinai: Yahweh makes the covenant with his people and the people promise to be faithful to him. The years in the desert are the time of the first love, when the bridegroom overwhelms his bride with favours and the bride follows her husband. One of the names often given to the people in its representation as Yahweh's bride is: daughter of

Zion or the maid Zion. However, Yahweh's bride gives signs of infidelity: she deserts Yahweh, runs after strange gods and commits adultery. Particularly the Prophets reproach the daughter of Zion for her unfaithfulness (cf. Hos. i–iii; Ezek. xvi): Yahweh will punish his unfaithful bride and send her into exile. But disaster and punishment are not his final word; a small remnant of the people will, purified and chastised by God's hand, repent and return from exile as a pure bride who has regained the true bearing of loyalty and complete surrender to Yahweh, her bridegroom. This faithful, deeply religious remnant of the people is often also called daughter of Zion by the Prophets; they invite the faithful daughter of Zion to rejoice because one day, in the messianic future, Yahweh will come to live among these faithful followers as King and as a redeeming, saving God. A few instances of prophecies which bring out this characteristic are: Zeph. iii.14–17; Zech. ix.9–10; Joel ii.21–7.

The opening words of the annunciation of the angel to Mary (Luke i.28–31) show a strong resemblance to those prophecies; the greatest and clearest link is with the passage from Zephaniah, which I quote insofar as it is important in this comparison with the passage from Luke:

Sing aloud, O daughter of Zion . . .
The King of Israel, the Lord, is [comes] in your midst . . .

On that day it shall be said to Jerusalem:
"Do not fear, O Zion . . .
The Lord, your God, is [comes] in your midst,
  a warrior who gives victory!"

This passage, we observe, is constructed from
two parallel verses, each preceded by an invitation
to messianic joy, "sing aloud" and the equivalent
"do not fear", and followed by the content of the
message which also gives the reason for this joy:
"The Lord comes in your midst as saviour" to
redeem his people, and "as King" to establish his
kingdom for ever. All the traits of these prophetic messages (we find the same with Zechariah
and Joel as we do in the probably older passage
from Zephaniah) are encountered in the messianic
message of joy *par excellence*, in Gabriel's annunciation to Mary in Luke i.28–31:

	i.28	
Hail,[52]	O favoured one,	the Lord is with you.

	i.30–31	
Do not be afraid, Mary,	for you have found favour with God.	And behold, you will conceive in your womb and bear a son, and you shall call his name Jesus.

Here, too, we have two parallel verses, introduced by "hail" and "do not be afraid"; a parallel,

moreover, which is carried through to "favoured one" (or "privileged one", "chosen one", "subject of God's pleasure") in i.28. In i.30 we see the corresponding "you have found favour with God"; then follows, in i.28: "the Lord is with you." This is not a promise of Yahweh's help and protection but an announcement of the presence of the Lord in her as in the prophecies quoted. Besides, this section from verse 28 is more closely defined and clarified in i.31 which runs parallel with the end of i.28 ("the Lord is with you"): this presence of the Lord with her, has its concrete realization in the fact that she will conceive in her womb and bring forth a son whose name she shall call Jesus. The presence of the Lord as the *saviour* of his people, spoken of by the prophetic texts, will be manifested in her motherhood of a child that is to receive the name Jesus (i.e., *Yahweh saves*). This child is the Lord who, in the words of the Prophets, would one day come among his people as *King*; for he will *reign* over the house of Jacob for ever; and of his kingdom there will be no end. (i.32–3.)

The connection between Luke i.28–31 and Zeph. iii.14–17 will have grown clearer in the meantime. But there is also a difference: Zephaniah addresses his prophetic message, prefaced by the invitation to gladness, to the daughter of Zion, to the faithful, religious, people which lays itself open entirely to Yahweh and submits to him like a devoted servant, whereas here the prophetic

message and this call to messianic joy are
addressed to Mary, God's chosen one, in whom at
this moment, on the threshold of the messianic
era, the joyful words of the Prophets to the
daughter of Zion are about to be fulfilled. She is
the daughter of Zion, the personification of the
faithful Israel, which opens out, as it were, in her.
She is the top of the pyramid formed by the
anavim or poor, who want to be Yahweh's
devoted servants. She is the epitome of the faithful
Israel which opens up completely for Yahweh
and surrenders unreservedly to him in the firm
conviction that salvation comes from him and
that he is able to fulfil the redemptive promises
against all human calculations. Entirely in con-
formity with this identification of Mary with the
daughter of Zion, the sacred author of the childhood story repeatedly presents her as the faithful
one; she gives the reply dictated by her faith:
"Behold, I am the handmaid of the Lord; let it
be to me according to your word." (i.38.) She
declares herself the devoted servant of God and
leaves him an entirely free hand. This answer that
wells up from the faith of this ordinary girl from
unknown Nazareth in despised Galilee is in
strong contrast in the structure of Luke i–ii with
the enforced silence of the disappointed, un-
believing, Zechariah, a priest in the religious
centre of the capital, Jerusalem. (i.20.) Her
Magnificat is a hymn of praise that rises from the
heart of an ordinary person who thanks God in

personal religious surrender for the wonderful
things he has done in her and places herself
entirely at the disposal of this active God. In
Mary's election and blessing, God came to
Israel's assistance, as expressed in the final verse
of the *Magnificat*: in accordance with his redemptive promises to the Fathers, he remembered his
mercy to Abraham and to his descendants for
ever. Just as Israel received the promises in the
person of Abraham, the father of the faithful, so
religious Israel, the daughter of Zion, accepts
those promises in the person of Mary, whose faithful bearing earns her the name of "mother of
the faithful". The redemptive history of the
people Israel commences with Abraham's act of
faith; the redemptive history of the New
Covenant is rung in by Mary's act of faith. Therefore she will be beatified by Elizabeth: "Blessed
is she who believed. . . ." (i.45.) The gospel's first
blessing will also be the last: "Blessed are those
who have not seen and yet believe." (John xx.29.)
Thus it was in the beginning, thus it is now, and
thus it will remain for all eternity.

Notes

1. W. Grossouw, in *Bijbels Woordenboek*, 2nd ed., col. 482–3.
2. Cf. Dom Charlier, in *Bible et Vie chrétienne*, no. 7 (1954), pp. 42–56; *La discrétion des Evangiles sur la Vierge*.
3. All ancient MSS and the oldest translations contain Matt. i–ii and Luke i–ii. From the second century onwards these chapters are quoted by the Fathers Justin and Irenaeus, and even by the heretic Cerinthus and the pagan Celsus.
4. Marie-Joseph Lagrange, *The Gospel of Jesus Christ*, London, Burns & Oates (1938), pp. 8–9.
5. Cf. the *excursus* "Die Eigenart und geschichtliche Glaubwürdigkeit der Kindheitsgeschichte des Matthäus", in J. Schmid, *Das Evangelium nach Matthäus*, 3rd ed., Regensburg (1956), pp. 53–5.
6. There is a very instructive article on the genealogy of Jesus according to Matthew in *H. Land* (1957), pp. 182–3.
7. Cf. A. Denis, OP, "De Aanbidding der Wijzen volgens Mattheus' visie", in *Tijdschrift voor Geestelijk Leven* (1957), pp. 713–23.
8. Cf. B. van Iersel, "Uit Egypte heb ik mijn zoon geroepen", in *H. Land* (1959), pp. 120–22.
9. Note in this connection the plural: "by the prophets"; elsewhere in Matt. i–ii we invariably find the singular: "by the prophet". (Matt. i.22–3; ii.5, 15, 17.)
10. The passages in which Matthew quotes prophecies that were fulfilled in Jesus are legion: Matt. iii.3;

iv.14–16; viii.17; xii.17–21; xiii.35; xxi.4ff; xxvi.56; xxvii.9ff., 35.

11. Cf. J. Keulers, *De Boeken van het Nieuwe Testament*, 2nd ed., Roermond (1951), vol. 2, pp. 145–6: "De geschiedkundige waarde van hfdst. 1 en 2 van Lucas"; cf. also "Die Eigenart und der geschichtliche Wert der Kindheitsgeschichte des Lukas und ihr Verhältnis zu der des Matthäus", in J. Schmid, *Das Evangelium nach Lukas*, 3rd ed., Regensburg (1955), pp. 84–91.

12. Codex D in Acts xi.28 reads: "when we were assembled"; if this version of the western text is correct, this is the first "we-fragment" (cf. Acts xvi.10–17; xx.5–xxi.18; xxvii.1–xxviii.16), from which it would appear that Luke was at that time a member of Antioch's Christian community.

13. Luke, who says in his prologue that he has carefully examined all things from the beginning, has certainly known and used Mark's Gospel and in all probability he has also known Matthew's Gospel in one "prototype" or another. He has also collated verbal information from the "disciples" who do not belong to the twelve, from the women who followed Jesus, from St Paul, from Jesus' relatives and from the circles around the apostle John.

14. Cf. Luke i.1–2: "... of the things which have been accomplished among us, just as they were delivered to us by those who from the beginning were eyewitnesses and ministers of the word."

15. A few statistical data: 548 verses—almost half of the 1149 verses that make up Luke's Gospel—belong to the so-called *Sondergut* of Luke: items which are peculiar to him and appear in neither Mark nor Matthew.

16. In justification of this "unusual" translation which is based mainly on an accurate appreciation of the contrast between *to gar* and *texetai de* in Matt. 1.20–21,

I refer to parallel constructions like Acts xiii.36ff.;
Matt. xviii.7; xxii.14; xxiv.6; John xx.17; cf. X. Léon-
Dufour, "L'annonce à Joseph", in *Mélanges Robert*,
Paris (1957), pp. 390–7. The implications of the peri-
cope under discussion will probably show up clearest
from the following translation and paraphrase:

i.18: Now the birth of Jesus Christ took place as
follows: when Mary, his mother, was betrothed to
Joseph, she was found to be with child through the
intervention of the Holy Ghost, before they started
living together. [I believe that Joseph was aware of
the mystery, not from personal observation but
through another's information; P. Gächter (pp. 113ff.)
thinks that Joseph had been appraised of the mystery
by the mother of Mary. In any event it seems out of
the question that Joseph suspects his bride of adultery;
and, moreover, the angel does not reveal this secret
to him in i.20ff.; he merely confirms what Joseph
already knows, though undecided what to do about
it.]

19: However, Joseph, her spouse, was a righteous
man [that is to say, he is fair to God; he wants to give
to God what is God's; he does not want to pass for
the father of a child conceived by his bride through
a special intervention from God] and would not give
her (secret) away. This is why he had formed the
idea to secretly leave her free. [That is, to leave her
free for God alone; he wants to withdraw because he
has come to realize that God apparently has other,
higher, plans for his bride which compel him to
revise his own marriage plans. Joseph reacts here like
all the righteous ones in the Scriptures do when they
realize they are facing God's presence or intervention.
(Cf. Moses in Exod. iii.1–6; Isaiah in Isa. vi; Peter in
Luke v.1–11.) In holy fear he wants to let God deter-
mine his own future as well as that of his chosen
bride.]

20: While he was harbouring this plan (or, when he had made his decision) behold, there appeared to him an angel of the Lord in a dream and he said to him: Joseph, son of David, be not afraid to take Mary, your spouse [do not hesitate to take Mary to you by the so-called "homing"];

21: for, though it is undoubtedly true that what is born in her is the work of God's Spirit [despite everything, you too have a task to fulfil, not in the conception of the child but at his birth, to wit]: she shall bring forth a son whom you [as legal father] must name Jesus; for he shall redeem his people from their sins.

22: Now, all this has taken place in fulfilment of the Lord's prophecy:

23: Behold, a virgin shall conceive and bear a son, whom they [that is, not only Mary, but Joseph also. Note that Matthew changes the wording of Isa. vii.14 here: by putting the verb "to call" in the third person plural his version of this prophecy from Isaiah indicates not only Mary's (and the Spirit's) task but also Joseph's as legal father in naming the child] must (shall) give the name Emmanuel, which means: God with us.

24: When he awoke from sleep, Joseph did as the angel of the Lord had commanded him: he took his wife [that is, he acted as legal husband and thus also as her child's legal father].

25: And without having any relations she brought forth a son; and she called this child Jesus.

17. Mic. v.3 reads: "Therefore he shall give them up until the time when she who is in travail has brought forth." The prophet Micah, who is a contemporary of Isaiah and has many points of contact with the great prophet in his book, doubtless refers to the *almah* (young woman) and the child mentioned in Isa. vii.14.

18. A few MSS of Luke ii.33 have the version "Joseph and his [Jesus'] mother" instead of "his father and mother"; apparently they want to avoid every possible misunderstanding about Joseph's fatherhood. There is a similar tendency in Luke ii.41–3.

19. Cf. *H. Land* (1956), pp. 2–6.

20. Cf. J. Schmid, pp. 44–50; B. van Iersel, "Gelovige Maagd", in *Standaard van Maria* (1956), pp. 213–14.

21. Cf. Luke iv.9–12 with Matt. iv.8–11: Luke transposes the third temptation to the pinnacles of the temple. Especially from ix.51 onwards, Jerusalem becomes predominant: after a solemn introduction we see here the beginning of the great narrative of the journey to Jerusalem (cf. xiii.22; xvii.11) that runs right through to xviii.14; cf. also xviii.31; xix.28, 41, 45. Even after the Resurrection all the events take place in Jerusalem or its surroundings. Unlike Matthew, Luke does not mention any apparitions of the risen Lord in Galilee.

22. The narrative of Matt. ii appears to have undergone the stylistic influence of an apocryphal Mosaic legend, traces of which are found, among others, in Flavius Josephus. According to this *midrash*, Pharaoh is startled when he learns of the birth of a saviour of Israel (cf. Herod in Matt. ii.3–4); he asks the learned men for information on the birthplace (cf. Matt. ii.4); Pharaoh orders the execution of the children (cf. Matt. ii.16); in a dream Moses' father is told that his son will be saved (cf. Matt. ii.13). In Matt. ii.20 the death of the persecutor is announced to Joseph in the words of Exod. iv.19. Generally speaking, this typifying of Jesus as the new Moses is characteristic of Matthew's Gospel. (Cf. the opening of the Sermon on the Mount; especially Matt. v.20–48.)

23. This chorus in Luke i.23 (i.e., towards the end of the first panel of the first diptych of the annunciations) says of Zechariah that "he went to his home"; similarly the end of the second panel of the

first diptych says of the angel that "he departed from her [Mary]". (i.38.) A like formula closes the narrative of the visitation in i.56: after a stay of about three months, Mary "returned to her home". We meet the same formula at the end of the second panel of the second diptych, in ii.20: "the shepherds returned"; after the presentation in the temple, we read in ii.39: "they returned into Galilee to their own city, Nazareth"; and finally, the scene of the finding in the temple, in ii.51, is closed with the observation that Jesus "went down with them and came to Nazareth".

24. We come across the chorus of the "growing-up" in i.80, i.e., as the conclusion of the first panel of the second diptych; almost the same formula is used about Jesus at the end of the narrative of the presentation in the temple, in ii.40; and we can read a variation of it in ii.51, after the story of the finding —a verse that looks like a combination of i.80 and ii.40. For this formula, cf. also Judges xiii.24 (Luke i.80; ii.40) and 1 Sam. ii.21–36; iii.19 (Luke ii.52). The passages quoted concern the childhood stories of Samson and Samuel, which show some likeness to the childhood stories of Jesus.

25. This chorus only occurs in Luke ii; at the end of the second panel of the second diptych, in ii.19, we read: "His mother kept all these things in her heart." This formula also concludes the childhood story in ii.51. This chorus has its antecedent in Dan. vii.28; cf. also Gen. xxxvii.11; 1 Sam. xxi.13.

26. Lyonnet speaks of "une sorte d'élargissement" (a kind of enlargement). (p. 5.)

27. I refer, among other stories, to that of the creation (Gen. i); cf. also the observations of Benoit in his introduction on Matthew's Gospel in the *Bible de Jérusalem*, p. 1287; cf. *Bijbels Woordenboek*, 2nd ed., col. 584ff.

28. Cf. P. Gächter, p. 58 and note 124.
29. It may well be that the author intends this antithetic parallelism to be his contribution to an ancient Christian controversy directed against remnants of Baptist sects who honoured John the Baptist as the Messiah. We could detect a similar controversy in John i.6–8: "There was a man sent from God, whose name was John. He came for testimony, to bear witness to the light, that all might believe through him. He was not the light, but came to bear witness to the light."
30. Cf. Tobit xiii.1; Ps. xlviii.2; lxxvi.2; lxxxvi.10; xcvi.4; cxxxv.5; cxlv.3; cxlvii.5; Jer. x.6.
31. Most exegetes repudiate the possibility that the author of the Book of Malachi was himself called Malachi. They hold that the title of the book—like that of Zech. ix–xi and xii–xiv—was originally anonymous; but the term *malaki* (my messenger) in iii.1 was conceived as the proper name of the one who was sent; this messenger was identified with the author of the Book of Malachi and thus the whole book was eventually ascribed to Malachi. The Septuagint does not yet understand this term as a proper name. Jewish tradition regards Malachi as the last (the "seal") of the Prophets.
32. The Malachi passage sees Elijah's task as the reconciliation of the families. Ecclus. xlviii.10 links up with this passage but depicts his task at the dawn of the messianic era as the restoration of Israel: "... to reconcile the heart of the father to the son and to restore the tribes of Israel." In Luke's passage the expression "the children" runs parallel with "the just". We might here think of a spiritual meaning: it is the little ones we read about in the gospel (Matt. x.42; xi.25; xviii.3, 10) who confidently await the eschatological restoration of the people.

Notes

33. Some authors think that the Johannine stories of Luke i–ii have had a separate prehistory and were originally detached from the childhood stories about Jesus. They also think these Johannine stories went back to disciples of the Baptist who felt little like subordinating their prophet to Jesus the Messiah. This might explain why the Messiah Jesus does not appear in the Johannine stories, where the Baptist is depicted as the forerunner of Yahweh the Lord, who will personally intervene. However this may be, the fact that Luke combines both cycles of narratives and subordinates the Baptist to the Messiah Jesus appears, nevertheless, to suggest that he views the Lord and the Messiah on the same plane. Jesus' coming to the temple, which is predicted in Malachi, he sees fulfilled in Jesus' entry into the temple. Cf. the remarks at the end of Chapter 3.

34. Cf. also the *invitatorium* (the bidding) to Matins, which takes the Malachi passage as the main theme of the feast: "Ecce, venit ad templum sanctum suum Dominator Dominus: gaude et laetare, Sion, occurrens Deo tuo." (Behold, the Lord comes to his holy temple: rejoice, O Zion, and run to your God with gladness.)

35. The Vulgate translates: "…et ut ungatur sanctus sanctorum" (…and he who is all holiness receives his anointing.)

36. The Book of Daniel has exerted an enormous influence and even Christendom has been considerably inspired by its apocalyptic literature. John's Apocalypse and Jesus' apocalyptic sermon in the Synoptic Gospels (Mark xiii; Matt. xxiv; Luke xxi) make lavish use of Daniel's themes. Jesus must have had the Book of Daniel constantly in mind. The proclamation of God's kingdom is the heart of his message; his most significant self-affirmation is that of the Son of Man. (Cf. Dan. vii.) The parable in Matt.

xiii is full of allusions to Daniel (cf. Matt. xiii.11, 32, 42–3); the hymn in Matt. xi.25ff. is reminiscent of Dan. ii.20–23. Peter's confession (Matt. xvi.17–19) makes us assume some familiarity with Daniel's work and the transfiguration is narrated on the lines of the theme of Dan. x. It should hardly surprise us therefore that Daniel's influence can also be felt in Luke's childhood story.

37. In this connection I draw attention to a remarkable coincidence. Luke i.5–ii.22 gives us a continuous chronology; according to Luke's data, six months elapse between Gabriel's messages to Zechariah and Mary (i.26, 36); we count nine months between the annunciation to Mary and the birth of Jesus in Bethlehem; forty days after the nativity there follows the presentation in the temple. (Cf. Lev. xii.3.) According to biblical practice, a month must be reckoned as thirty days; therefore between Gabriel's first appearance in the temple, at the annunciation to Zechariah, and the presentation of Jesus in the temple there is an interval of 490 days or seventy weeks. Possibly Luke saw in this remarkable chronological agreement with the seventy weeks mentioned in Dan. ix.24 a "miniature" fulfilment of the messianic prophecy of the seventy weeks which Gabriel made to Daniel. The revelation of Jesus in the temple, seventy weeks after Gabriel's first message, to Zechariah, is a fulfilment of Daniel's prophecy: the Holy of Holies is anointed in the temple of Jerusalem. I do not want to overemphasize this coincidence; the link between Luke i–ii and Dan. viii–ix and the meaning which the leading thought of Luke i–ii derives from it, are sufficiently firm without involving the chronology of the seventy weeks. Besides, it will be difficult to establish whether this is pure coincidence or a studied use on Luke's part of this chronology in his childhood story. It is nevertheless

a fact that elements of Daniel's prophecy of the seventy weeks are often the basis of certain messianic reflections. Thus the half week (three and a half years) of Dan. ix.27 (cf. Dan. vii.25; xii.7: "a time, two times and half a time") recurs in Rev. xi.3 in the form of 1260 days; in Rev. xiii.5 as forty-two months; cf. also Rev. xii.14: "a time, and times and half a time." Luke himself seems familiar with it, for in Luke iv.25 we read: "But in truth, I tell you, there were many widows in Israel in the days of Elijah, when the heaven was shut up three years and six months, when there came a great famine over all the land"; here Luke defines the passage of 1 Kings xviii.1 which speaks of "in the third year" as "three years and six months" because, since the persecution by King Antioch IV, this period has become synonymous with a period of disaster and misery, as in the passages from Daniel quoted. Cf. also Jas. v.17.

38. Cf. K. Schelkle, *De Bijbel over Maria*, Roermond, Romen and Zonen (1960), pp. 48ff.

39. The question is whether we can read Luke ii.19, 51 as a reference of the author to confidential information from Mary about the childhood of Jesus. The expression "to keep in one's heart" is a set formula and often occurs in apocalyptic literature. After Joseph has narrated his dream (Gen. xxxvii), the story goes, his brothers hated him more than ever. Even his father Jacob reprimanded him, but in contrast with the jealousy of his brothers, his father is said to have "kept the word". (xxxvii.11.) At the end of Dan. vii, which describes Daniel's vision of the Son of Man and its interpretation, he says: "Here is the end of the matter. As for me, Daniel, my thoughts greatly alarmed me, and my colour changed; but I kept the matter in my mind." (vii.28.) There is a similar situation in the Greek translation of Dan. iv.25; after the interpretation of the dream about the

colossal tree that has to be hewn down: "When Nebuchadnezzar had heard the interpretation of the dream, he kept the words in his heart." The "keeping of the words" invariably links up with the interpretation of the vision. Cf. Dan. viii.26; x.14; xii.4, 9; also 2 Esdras xiv.8 ". . . the dreams which you have seen and the interpretation which you have heard, keep them in your heart." The expression "to keep the words in the heart" is therefore part of the apocalyptic theme and is repeatedly used as a technical formula following the vision of a messianic enthronement, to be retained until its fulfilment. Cf. Neirynck, "De Kerstboodschap van Lucas", in *De Bazuin* (23 December, 1959), pp. 13ff.

40. Cf. Neirynck, pp. 6ff.

41. Cf. G. Bouwman, "Het Kindheidsevangelie van Lucas", in *Ned. Kath. Stemmen* (1959), pp. 289–98; especially p. 293.

42. Cf. R. Bloch, art Midrash, in *Dict. Bibl. Suppl.*, vol. V, col. 1263–81.

43. Pp. 7ff.

44. "L'Annonce à Marie", *Rev. Bibl.* 63 (1956), pp. 346–74.

45. In Audet's view, Mary knows that, according to the prophecy of Isa. vii.14, the Messiah will be born of a virgin. She herself is already betrothed; therefore, her query in Luke i.34 should be translated as follows: "How can this be, since in that case [i.e., if I were to become the mother of the Messiah] I would not be allowed to have a husband?"

46. *L'Enfance de Jean-Baptiste selon Luc i* (New Test. Stud.), vol. III (1956–7), pp. 169–94.

47. Pp. 43ff.

48. Cf. Bouwman, p. 297. The author only accepts the *midrash* character in respect of the annunciations. This seems to me too narrow a limitation; the vision of the shepherds has the same character as the appear-

ances of the angel in Luke i and evolves on similar lines. Cf. Neirynck, pp. 10–11.

49. R. Schnackenburg in *Theologisch Perspectief*, vol. I, p. 149.

50. Burrows, *The Gospel of the Infancy and other Biblical Essays*, London (1950), pp. 56ff.

51. Literally it says: "in your womb", but the expression is so hackneyed in Hebrew that Zephaniah is unlikely to have thought of the womb of the daughter of Zion. In his mind, Yahweh's coming "among" the people probably means that he comes to reside as Saviour and as Redeemer.

52. The translation "hail" seems more accurate than "greetings" and accords with the ancient Greek tradition which sees the angel as a prophetic figure that delivers the messianic message in a loud voice and calls for gladness. The *Petrus Canisius* translation adds "blessed art thou among women" to this verse, but this is wrong; in a few MSS these words seem to have found their way here from Luke i.42 (Mary's greeting by Elizabeth). Cf. Lyonnet in *Biblica*, 20 (1939), pp. 131–41.